Brief Coping Cat:
Therapist Manual for the
8-Session Workbook

Philip C. Kendall, Ph.D., ABPP

Sarah A. Crawley, Ph.D.
Courtney L. Benjamin, Ph.D.
Christian F. Mauro, Ph.D.

Workbook Publishing offers evidence-based child and adolescent workbooks, treatment manuals, and training materials.

Available are

- DVDs for training in the provision of the intervention programs and treatments.
- An interactive computer-assisted program (*Camp Cope-A-Lot*) to address anxiety in youth.
- Materials for youth with depression, anger management issues, and impulsivity.
- Materials for *EMOTION*, a group program for both anxiety and depression, that has compatible materials for working with parents.
- Materials for anxiety in youth, including child anxiety (*Coping cat program*; *Brief Coping cat program*) and anxiety in adolescents (*C.A.T. Project*).

Brief Coping Cat:
Therapist Manual for the
8-Session Workbook

Philip C. Kendall, Ph.D., ABPP

Sarah A. Crawley, Ph.D.
Courtney L. Benjamin, Ph.D.
Christian F. Mauro, Ph.D.

Brief coping cat: THERAPIST MANUAL FOR THE 8-SESSION WORKBOOK

Copyright © 2013
by Workbook Publishing, Inc.

ISBN: 978-1-888805-49-9

Printed in the United States of America

Workbook Publishing, Inc.
P.O. Box 67
Ardmore, PA 19003 USA
info@workbookpublishing.com

Précis and Acknowledgements

This therapist manual has three sections. In the first, the program is introduced in an overview fashion, with a discussion of issues related to the implementation of manual-based treatment with clinical flexibility. The second section contains detailed descriptions of the specific treatment sessions. A series of notes, or tips, from experienced therapists (referred to as "Tips from the Trenches") are appended to each of the treatment sessions in the form of a bullet-list with the main idea of each tip printed in bold. Based on research and clinical input, section three provides therapist resources for dealing with comorbid concerns and addressing complicating factors that may impact treatment success (e.g., family difficulties).

This therapist manual could not have been completed without the input and cooperation of numerous therapists and diagnosticians[1]. These individuals include my coauthors on the first edition, Drs. Martha Kane, Bonnie Howard, and Lynne Siqueland, who were invaluable in assisting in the initial organization of the manual, and the many other collaborators who have had input into the procedures now described herein: Drs. Anne Marie Albano, Rinad Beidas, Erika Brady, Tamar Chansky, Muniya Choudhury, Brian Chu, Ellen Flannery-Schroeder, Elizabeth Gosch, Aude Henin, Jennifer Hudson, Elizabeth Kortlander, Amy Krain, Jennefer Panas MacDonald, Abbe Garcia, Suzie Panichelli-Mindel, Sandra Pimentel, Jennifer Podell, Kevin Ronan, Fran Sessa, Michael Southam-Gerow, Cynthia Suveg, Kim Treadwell, Melissa Warman, and Alicia Webb. These therapists and others (i.e. Aleta Angelosante, Lindsey Bergman, Jonathan Comer, Alicia Hughes, Jennifer Jones, Joanna Robin, and Timothy Verduin) provided suggestions for the "Tips from the Trenches" that are provided at the end of each session. Other CBT therapists, such as those participating in the CAMS multi-site evaluation of treatments for anxiety disorders in youth (i.e., Walkup et al, 2008), my international colleagues working on translated versions of the treatment manuals and materials, and those who have interacted with me during conferences and workshops, are also thanked for their suggestions and interest. Special thanks to the numerous graduate students who provided feedback (e.g., Jami Furr; Erica Sood), who help to keep the manual alive, and who recently rose to the list of doctoral colleagues (above). Kristi Hedtke, my coauthor on the *Coping Cat* second edition, is singled out for her energetic efforts to improve the information in both the workbook and therapist manual. Collectively, all are thanked as is anyone whom we may have inadvertently omitted. Finally, appreciation is expressed to the many anxious children and their parents who have participated in the program over the years.

The development of this treatment program and its research evaluation have gone hand in hand. Preparation of this work was facilitated by and evaluated a research grants from the National Institute of Mental Health (e.g., MH080788).

---

[1] We would like to extend a special thank you to the expert reviewers of this manual for their thoughtful feedback: Anne Marie Albano, Ph.D., ABPP; John Piacentini, Ph.D., ABPP; Wendy Silverman, Ph.D.; John Walkup, M.D.

Introduction
Cognitive-Behavioral Therapy for Anxious Children

This treatment manual describes an 8-session program for the treatment of anxiety disorders, specifically for generalized anxiety disorder, social phobia, and separation anxiety disorder, in children and young adolescents.[2] The overall approach is cognitive-behavioral; an integration of the demonstrated efficacies of the behavioral approach (e.g., exposure tasks, relaxation training, role play activities, practice and reward) with an added emphasis of the cognitive information-processing factors associated with each individual's anxieties (anxious self-talk, emotional distress, anticipatory dread). Social forces (e.g., peers, families) are also included, as are emotion understanding and emotion management skills. The approach represents a rational amalgam and is a condensed, brief version of the 16-session program (Kendall & Hedke, 2006a).

The overall goal is to teach children to recognize signs of unwanted anxious arousal and to let these signs serve as cues for the use of anxiety management strategies. Identifying the cognitive processes associated with excessive anxious arousal, training in cognitive strategies for anxiety management, training in behavioral relaxation, and performance-based practice opportunities are sequenced within the manual to build skill upon skill. The greatest emphasis within the treatment program is placed upon the following general strategies:

> ➢ graduated sequence of training tasks and assignments
> ➢ role play procedures
> ➢ coping modeling
> ➢ homework assignments ("Show-That-I-Can"—STIC tasks)
> ➢ affective education
> ➢ awareness of bodily reactions when anxious
> ➢ relaxation training
> ➢ identification and modification of anxious self-talk
> ➢ contingent rewards
> ➢ practice of newly acquired skills in increasingly anxiety-provoking situations (i.e., exposure tasks), both imaginal and *in-vivo*

The strategies described herein are specifically coordinated with the *Brief Coping Cat Workbook (*Kendall, Beidas, & Mauro, 2010*)*, an abbreviated version of the *Coping Cat Workbook* (Kendall, 2000; Kendall & Hedtke, 2006b). The client workbook contains exercises and tasks consistent with the information presented and discussed in the treatment and in the manual. They go hand-in-hand and are meant to be used together.

---

[2] Although the manual is appropriate for young adolescents, the word "child" will be used in referring to the client. Readers interested in treating older adolescents are referred to the C.A.T. Project Manual (Kendall, Choudhury, Hudson, & Webb, 2002; www.WorkbookPublishing.com). Also, to increase the readability, the pronoun "he" will be used instead of "he/she" (himself/herself) to refer to the client and "she" to refer to the therapist.

The 8-session program is divided into two parts: The first sessions are the training segment and the second series of sessions are the practice (exposure tasks) segment. Two meetings between the therapist and the parent(s) (or one or more of the child's guardians) are scheduled at session 1 and session 4. The theory that guides the treatment is described in Kendall (1993; 2006). A 16-session version of the treatment is available (Kendall & Hedke, 2006a). For those interested in working within a family therapy context, see the therapist manual for family therapy for anxious children (Howard, Chu, Krain, Marrs-Garcia, & Kendall, 2000; Howard & Kendall, 1996; see also Fauber & Kendall, 1992). For those who wish to work in groups, see the therapist manual for group treatment (Flannery-Schroeder & Kendall, 1996). For more information about therapist manuals and treatment materials, consult the web (www.WorkbookPublishing.com).

Use of modeling, role-play, and between-session practice: Throughout the treatment, concepts and skills are introduced in a sequential order from basic to more difficult. The therapist functions as a model as the new skills are introduced—demonstrating not only the skill for the child, but also the difficulties that might be experienced and the strategies to overcome the difficulties. The therapist demonstrates first in each new situation. The child is invited to participate with the therapist in role plays, using a "tag-along" procedure (see Ollendick & Cerny, 1981). Finally, the child is encouraged to role play scenes alone, practicing newly acquired skills. Within each session and throughout the training program, the level of anxiety is gradually increased, beginning with the non-stressful situations and gradually incorporating increasing levels of anxiety. "Show-That-I-Can" (STIC) tasks are assigned as tasks to be completed outside of the therapy setting to help show the applicability of what has been addressed during the session.

Key therapeutic concepts: Several important concepts are sequentially introduced to the child during the training segment of the program, beginning with the awareness of bodily reactions to feelings and developing recognition of those reactions that are specific to anxiety (coordinated with client assignments in the *Brief Coping Cat Workbook*). The child is trained to use physical reactions as a cue to the presence of anxiety. Anxious children lack skills associated with understanding their ability to modify their emotions (Southam-Gerow & Kendall, 2000), so these limitations are addressed in treatment. The next general concept that is introduced to the child is learning to recognize and modify his anxious "self-talk" (see Kendall & MacDonald, 1993; Ronan, Kendall & Rowe, 1994; Treadwell & Kendall, 1996). Both his expectations and fears about what will happen and the role he sees for himself in the situation are important. The third concept presented to the child is the modification of his anxious self-talk into coping self-talk and developing plans for coping with his anxieties more effectively in different situations. The fourth concept introduced to the child is self-rating and reward—reward for effort!

The 4-step FEAR plan: These four concepts are summarized in a 4-step plan for coping with anxiety. To help facilitate the child's recall of the plan, an acronym will be introduced. The acronym forms the FEAR plan, with each letter of FEAR standing for a step in the plan:

4

Feeling **F**rightened?
Expecting bad things to happen?
Attitudes and **A**ctions that can help
Results and **R**ewards

Behavioral rehearsal and exposure tasks: The second segment of the program is devoted to the application and practice of the newly acquired knowledge and skills in increasingly anxiety provoking situations. The same training strategies are employed, including coping modeling, role play activities, and STIC assignments. The situations that are presented to each child are individually designed for him based on his own particular fears and worries (see Kendall et al., 2005a). The first practice sessions involve in-office exposure tasks, associated with low levels of anxiety and are followed by actual, *in-vivo* experiences in low stress situations. Subsequent sessions involve repeating this process in situations that are even more stressful for the child, helping the child to master his skills by exposing him to a number of different anxiety-provoking situations. Finally, the last session gives the child an opportunity to share and show off what he has learned with others.

Evidence supporting treatment efficacy: It is worth noting that the 16 session version of this treatment (Kendall & Hedke, 2006a) has been evaluated in several randomized clinical trials with one-year follow-up data conducted both in the United States (e.g., Kendall, 1994; Kendall et al., 1997) and in Australia (e.g., Barrett, Dadds & Rapee, 1996). The outcomes have been favorable; with 3.35 year-follow-up of one study (Kendall & Southam-Gerow, 1996) and 7.4 year-year follow-up of the second study (Kendall, Safford, Flannery-Schroeder, & Webb, 2004) providing evidence of the maintenance of gains. In conjunction with the criteria recommended for use in determination of treatments that qualify as having been supported by empirical research (Chambless & Hollon, 1998), reviewers of the literature indicate that the 16 session treatment is empirically-supported (see Kazdin & Weisz, 1998; Ollendick & King, 1998; Ollendick, King, & Chorpita, 2006; Silverman, Pina, & Viswesvaran, 2008).

A note about this brief treatment: This program was adapted from the 16 session Coping Cat using knowledge from the empirical literature, clinical experiences collected by therapists at the Child and Adolescent Anxiety Disorders Clinic, and input from a panel of experts in the field of child anxiety. The essential components of the FEAR plan have been retained, requiring minor modifications to the organization of the program. For example, the "F" and "E" steps are presented in a single session, and the "A" and "R" steps have also been condensed into a single session. The adaptations reduce or eliminate content in some areas (e.g. relaxation, end of treatment commercial), enabling therapists to cover essential content in a shorter time span. These modifications are consistent with efforts to reduce the length of treatment and provide optimal care. Nevertheless, they may not be appropriate for certain children, such as those who are in families with high levels of parental psychopathology or family dysfunction or children who have significant cognitive deficits. Other children/families may benefit from supplemental sessions to build rapport (if extreme social anxiety) and/or work on parenting techniques.

Readers interested in more details about specific topics may find leads in the following suggestions. Discussion of a broad range of topics related to the treatment of anxious youth is presented in Kendall and Holmbeck (1991); Kendall, Hudson, Choudhury, Webb, and Pimentel (2005b); and Kendall and Treadwell (1996). Issues related to the transportability of the treatment from the research setting to the service clinic appears in Kendall and Southam-Gerow (1995) and Hudson, Krain, and Kendall (2001). Information about the computer-assisted treatment program, *Camp Cope-A-Lot* (Kendall & Khanna, 2008), can be found at www.WorkbookPublishing.com, and data on its outcomes appear in Khanna and Kendall (in press). Evidence regarding the applicability of the treatment across changing diagnostic criteria appears in Kendall and Warman (1996) and across ethnicity and gender appears in Treadwell, Flannery, and Kendall (1995). Readers interested in additional data with regard to the treatment are encouraged to consult the following sources: Regarding process variables, see Chu and Kendall (2004) and Creed and Kendall (2005); regarding maternal expectations and attributions about coping in anxious youth, see Kortlander, Kendall, and Panichelli-Mindel (1997); regarding the social expectations and self-perceptions of anxious youth, see Chansky and Kendall (1997); regarding flexibility within fidelity, see Kendall & Chu (2000) and Kendall, Gosch, Furr, & Sood (2008); and regarding randomized clinical trails demonstrating efficacy, see Kendall, Hudson, Gosch, Flannery-Schroeder, and Suveg (2008) and Walkup et al. (2008). For suggestions and specific considerations of strategies related to the exposure tasks, see Kendall, Robin, Hedtke, Gosch, Flannery-Schroeder, and Suveg, (2005a). A description of the Child and Adolescent Anxiety Disorders Clinic and its services can be found online (www.childanxiety.org) and appears in Kendall et al. (2005b). Examples of case applications can be found in Suveg, Comer, Furr, and Kendall (2006) and Krain, Hudson, Coles, and Kendall (2002), and discussions of developmental, familial, and related topics can be found in the Special Issue of the *International Journal of Cognitive Psychotherapy* (2006) and in the Special Issue of *Cognitive and Behavioral Practice* (vol. 11, 2004). Two recent reports, appearing in *Cognitive and Behavioral Practice*, include video samples of treatment components (see Beidas, Benjamin, Puleo, Edmunds, & Kendall, 2010; Podell, Mychailyszyn, Edmunds, Puleo, & Kendall, 2010). See the appendix at the end of this manual for suggested treatment modifications for children presenting with comorbidity.

Flexibility within Fidelity

Treatment manuals should be guiding templates, not rigid cookbooks. In the pages that follow, we have organized and sequenced the strategies described in the introduction to help youth manage and overcome anxious distress. The approach is structured, but good clinical skills and therapist flexibility are needed to individualize the program for each child's specific needs—to maximize gains.

Therapists working within manual-based treatment programs are referred to an article entitled "Breathing life into a manual" which provides discussion of several ways to be manual-based and flexible in the provision of treatment services (Kendall, Chu, Gifford, Hayes, & Nauta, 1999). Therapists are not only exposed to the strategies of a specified intervention program, but also make necessary adjustments to have the program be a "good fit" for each child and his family. Therapy certainly benefits from therapist sensitivity to (a) comorbid conditions, (b) developmental level, (c) familial and environmental stressors, (d) socioeconomic status, and (e) home and school functioning.

With knowledge of such individual differences, the following treatment program is applied flexibly, but within fidelity--modifying cognitive and/or behavioral components of the treatment to best help the particular child. In other words, the therapist focuses on the purpose and goals of the session and modifies the tasks/activities to fit the needs of each individual child (see Kendall & Chu, 2000; Kendall et al., 2008). For example, a client might benefit from additional parental support, so parents might be encouraged to join the child during sessions. Another client might have an upcoming anxiety provoking situation (e.g. a spelling test, doctor's visit, or school event). The therapist should address these concerns while ensuring they leave enough time to accomplish the main session goals.

To enhance flexibility, therapists should familiarize themselves with the session content prior to beginning each session. Some children will need more time on some session goals (e.g. a shy child that needs more rapport building prior to the discussion of anxious feelings) and less time on others. The therapist should balance the child's needs with the session goals such that all goals are met within each session.

To encourage therapists to apply the treatment flexibly, but within fidelity, we included a feature from the second edition of the *Coping Cat* treatment manual. Embedded within the session content, "call-outs," such as the one presented below point to activities or content that can be modified to flexibly meet a child's needs.

FLEX

Although all session activities described in the manual (not just the ones that are tagged) can be implemented flexibly, our hope is that the "F L E X" call-out will (a) serve as a reminder for therapists to remain flexible when presenting treatment content and (b) help therapists select an activity or content that lends itself easily to flexible use. In addition to the call-out, we also include suggestions from actual therapists, listed herein as "Tips from the Trenches." These, too, are intended to be flexible and helpful suggestions.

The following pages contain session-by-session descriptions that detail the features of the treatment. In each instance a statement of the overall purpose of the session is presented followed by an outline of the specific goals and tasks. Although not intended as a transcript of the treatment, the manual was designed to serve as a guiding template for the integration and application of the treatment strategies for the treatment of youth anxiety. For additional materials for training and implementation, please see DVD entitled "CBT4CBT", available from the publisher (Kendall & Khanna, 2008). Additionally, Beidas, Podell, and Kendall (2008) provide helpful suggestions for session by session implementation.

This manual was developed for use by therapists from varied training backgrounds and differing levels of expertise. Our goal was to develop a manual-based treatment that could be effectively applied by the wide-range of treatment providers charged with providing care to youth with anxiety. Thus, individuals with a great deal of experience implementing cognitive-behavioral therapy and/or working with anxious youth might find some of the examples and tips to be elementary. Others with more limited experience may find it necessary to seek out additional training and/or resources to implement this treatment.

Table of Contents

Table of Contents Cont.

Building Rapport, Treatment Orientation, and the First Parent Meeting
Session 1

Purpose

Get to know one another. Go "easy" and don't focus on anxiety. Make it pleasant so the child wants to return for Session 2. Explain basic information about the program. Begin to gather information about situations that make the child anxious and the child's reactions to feelings of anxiety. Help the child identify different types of feelings and to distinguish anxious/worried feelings from other types of feelings. Encourage parental cooperation in the treatment program. Answer parents' questions.

Goals

Child session (60 minutes)

1. Build rapport – have fun, play, and make it easy for the child so that the child will want to return
2. Orient child to the program
3. Normalize anxiety
4. Encourage and support the child's participation
5. Introduce the concept that different feelings have different physical expressions
6. Introduce the concept of an anxiety hierarchy and the feelings thermometer
7. Assign an initial simple Show-That-I-Can (STIC) task
8. Engage in a fun end-of-session activity

Parent session (30 minutes)

1. Provide additional information about the treatment program
2. Learn more about the situations in which the child becomes anxious
3. Offer specific ways the parents can be involved in the program
4. Provide parents with a copy of the *Parent Companion* (Kendall, Podell & Gosch, 2010)

Tasks (Child Session)

1.   Build rapport

➢   It is essential that the therapist not move too quickly. Anxious children are often avoidant, generally fearful or wary, and typically not familiar with our inquiries about their feelings, beliefs, or attitudes. Rapport between the anxious child and the therapist is critical to success, and it is certainly worthwhile to devote ample time to the establishment of a trusting relationship between the child and therapist.

➢   Opening conversation

The first several minutes are for opening conversation: <u>no focus</u>, <u>no threat</u>. The therapist asks the child to make himself at home, look around the room, try any of the toys or games he'd like, and encourages the child to suggest a fun activity for the end of the hour. The therapist has suggestions of possible activities if the child has difficulty naming one. When the child has become somewhat involved and has selected an activity for the end of the session, the therapist can then agree in a manner something like the following: "Ok, that would be fun to do. Let's be sure to save 5-10 minutes to do that together." The therapist checks a watch and notes the time. Trust is built on reliable recall of the "deal" and sticking to it.

➢   Get to know each other

To introduce the therapist's need to gather information, and the idea that this information is important to the therapist, play a "Personal Facts" game (you can use pp. 1-2 in the *Brief Coping Cat Workbook* as a guide). In this game both the child and therapist supply answers to the same questions, such as "What is your middle name?" "How old are you?" "How many brothers and sisters do you have?" etc. In addition, including questions about favorite TV shows, videogames, music, heroes, and superheroes can provide information that will be helpful later in the treatment. After giving answers, the therapist and child playfully quiz each other on the answers, with a small prize going to the players (i.e., provide a reward for participating in question answering). It is important that the therapist recall

12

the information accurately, as this information is one of the child's first attempts to share personal data with the therapist. It is suggested that the therapist be comfortable with the child's asking personal information and with providing answers to appropriate questions.

2.   **<u>Orient child to the program</u>**

> Give a brief overview of the program (e.g., meeting each week) and create the sense that this program is a joint effort (collaborative) between the therapist and child.

> Provide a review of the reasons for the program ("Helps some kids with..."). Ask the child, "What is your understanding of why you are here?" or "What are the top things you want to work on?" It is important for the therapist to avoid being "preachy" and begin the process of collaboration between the child and therapist.

> Mention the goals for the program, including being able to identify anxious feelings, recognize anxious thoughts, and use appropriate coping strategies. These ideas are introduced as "knowing when you're anxious" and "knowing what to do about it"—with the focus of the first few sessions on "knowing when you're anxious," followed by sessions that will focus on "knowing what to do about it."

> Work with the child to identify specific treatment goals such as "sleep over at a friend's house" or "go to camp this summer." Keep in mind the brief duration of treatment and make sure to set realistic goals that are feasible within this time frame. One or two specific goals ("deliverables") are generally more feasible to accomplish than a multitude of goals or a vague goal ("worry less").

> Provide a brief overview of each of the FEAR steps. Explain that the child will learn each of these in more detail later. Explain to the child that the FEAR steps are the 4-step plan he will be learning to cope with his anxiety and teach him what the 4 steps stand for.

13

Feeling **F**rightened?
Expecting bad things to happen?
Attitudes and **A**ctions that can help
Results and **R**ewards

3.   **Normalize the experience of anxiety**

> Initiate a discussion to reassure the child that all people have fears and anxieties (including adults who are admired as brave or labeled as heroes) and that the purpose of this program is to help him learn to recognize distress and cope with it effectively. We ALL feel anxious at various times, but some of us are better than others at knowing what to do when it happens. Some of us are better at "regulating" the emotion, like adjusting the volume on the radio. The skills to deal with anxiety can be learned, just like learning to ride a bike or roller blade. The purpose of the program is to help the child learn and use the skills to manage anxious feelings.

> The therapist provides a coping model, disclosing a prior fear or situation which made her feel anxious. How it felt, how it was uncomfortable at first, and how it was handled are included in the disclosure.

4.   **Encourage/support the child's participation**

> Invite the child's questions about the treatment and re-open the invitation periodically until the child begins to share his questions and concerns.

> Ask the child to tell some stories of fun activities, family trips, or school events that were particularly enjoyable. Reward participation, encourage verbalization, and ask easy-to-answer questions.

> Point out that different people see things differently (Provide concrete examples such as "A brick wall that is very tall to a child may be small to a full-grown and tall man." "A tasty treat for one person may be the cause of an upset stomach for someone else."). Emphasize that we're interested in "What *you* see and think about various situations."

14

5. <u>**Briefly introduce the concept that different feelings have different physical expressions**</u> ~~FLEX~~

➢ Discuss different feelings

Discuss the idea that people's bodies can do different things in response to different feelings, and that different facial expressions and postures are clues to their feelings. The therapist can have the child list as many feelings as he can think of in the *Brief Coping Cat Workbook* (p.3), and try to assess which feelings the child is most comfortable talking about.

6. <u>**Introduce the concept of constructing a hierarchy of anxiety-provoking situations**</u>

➢ Introduce the Feelings Thermometer: Subject Units of Distress Scale (SUDS)

The thermometer uses a scale ranging from 0-8:

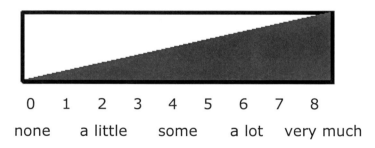

0	1	2	3	4	5	6	7	8
none		a little		some		a lot	very much	

This scale can be used to help determine which situations are more anxiety provoking for the child. The therapist asks the question: "How much anxiety do you feel when _____?" "Give it a number."

➢ Explain that you and the child will construct a hierarchy. Inform the child that throughout treatment the therapist and child will discuss the specifics of the child's anxieties, including the types of situations that provoke anxiety, the child's reactions to anxiety (somatic and cognitive), and the child's response in the anxiety-provoking situations. The therapist and child will note these situations and possibly use them later on to practice the skills the child is learning.

➢ Begin to discuss specific situations the child experiences as anxiety-provoking if the child is comfortable doing so. Some children are ready to begin this discussion in the first session while others are not yet comfortable. Don't force children to discuss their own anxiety before they are ready as it can detract from building a solid therapeutic relationship.

7. **Assign an initial simple Show-That-I-Can (STIC) task**

➢ To introduce out-of-session activities, the child is told that Show-That-I-Can (STIC) tasks are assigned and reviewed at each meeting. For the first STIC task, give the child the *Brief Coping Cat Workbook* and ask him (a) to bring the workbook to the next session and (b) to write in it a brief example of a time when he feels really great—not upset or worried. The child is asked to focus on what made him comfortable and what he thought at that time. To help the child understand the assignment, the therapist provides an example of a time when she felt really great and describes what she thought. Then the child is given a chance to do the same.

➢ The child is told he can earn 2 points (or stickers for younger children) at the next meeting to be entered in the "bank" on page 51 of the *Brief Coping Cat Workbook* for having completed the STIC task. If a child does not complete the STIC task at home, but does in session, a single point may be awarded. If the STIC task is not done, no points are entered. The points earned are used to purchase rewards periodically during the program (after Sessions 2, 4, 6, and 8). The child can select the rewards he wants to earn and enter them in the "reward menu" on page 52 of the *Brief Coping Cat Workbook*. Rewards should be developmentally appropriate and of interest to the child. Options for rewards can be small toys, books, games, or social rewards such as time spent playing a computer game with the therapist or going out for a treat (e.g., ice cream).

8. **Engage in fun end-of-session activity**

➢ After the session content has been addressed, take 8-10 minutes to play a game or engage in an activity (e.g., looking up something on the internet, telling funny stories, talking about episodes of favorite TV shows) that was selected with the child at the beginning of the session. Engaging in a fun activity serves several purposes. Foremost, it's fun! When a child views participation as a potentially fun and a positive experience, he will be more likely to want to attend subsequent sessions and engage in session activities. Also, engaging in the fun activity that had been selected at the start of the session shows the child that the therapist "follows-through:" helping to establish trust. Finally, playing a game or engaging in a fun activity at the end of session is a reward for the child's attendance and effort in the session.

Tasks (Parent Session)

1. **<u>Provide additional information about the treatment program</u>**
    *   The therapist outlines the treatment program and explains (generally) what the child will be doing. Parents' questions are invited and answered. The therapist reminds the parents that the first segment of the treatment is learning skills and that reduction in anxiety is not an overnight occurrence and may not be apparent until the child begins to learn to apply coping skills during the second half of the treatment.

    *   Invite parents to discuss their concerns about the child or about other factors that could affect the child's difficulties and ability to benefit from the treatment. With open-ended questions, the therapist invites the parents to provide any additional history or current information which they feel will be helpful to the therapist in understanding the child. Keep this part of the session **time-limited** (e.g., 10 minutes).

2. **<u>Learn more about the situations in which the child becomes anxious</u>**
    *   Using what has been learned in the first session, the therapist talks generally about her impressions of situations that are troublesome for the child and of the child's typical somatic and cognitive responses to anxiety. She invites the parents to share their impressions.
    *   Identify one or two specific behaviors to target during the intervention period (i.e., "deliverables"). Keep in mind the child and parent's preferences when deciding up on these goals.

3. **<u>Offer specific ways the parents can be involved in the program</u>**
    *   The therapist provides the parents with a copy of the BCBT Parent Companion and recommends that they read about the content of each session weekly.

    *   The therapist invites the parents to call the therapist if they have any questions, or if they think of additional information that they would like the

therapist to know. Depending on the age of the child and the quality of parental support, the therapist may ask for the parents' help in specific areas during the coming weeks, such as helping to define the hierarchy, monitoring the child's progress, and encouraging and rewarding the child's efforts. This is also a good opportunity to review logistics, discuss confidentiality with parents, and schedule the next session.

4. **Provide the parents with a copy of the _Parent Companion_**

    ➢ The therapist introduces the parents to the _Parent Companion_ (Kendall et al., 2010) and suggests that they follow the child's progress weekly. Parents are reminded that they play an important role in the child's treatment.

To help browse the tips with ease, the main idea/topic of each tip is in **bold**. This formatting applies to each session's "Tips from the Trenches."

Child Session

➢ **Try to make the first session fun!** Playing a game at the beginning and/or end of the session or giving the child a "tour" of the clinic can help ease the child's fears about commencing treatment. Keep in mind that the tone of therapy is set in this session – the therapist should set expectations that that the child will be reinforced for progress towards goals in therapy. The therapist may explain that one of today's goals is to get to know each other and indicate that the games help accomplish this goal.

➢ **Proceed slowly** because the therapy situation alone is one that provokes anxiety, and the therapist often becomes another person that the child feels he has to please.

➢ It is useful for the therapist to **have or gain knowledge of the child's interests** (i.e., likes and dislikes) prior to the first session. Knowing a little bit about the child shows the child that the therapist is interested in getting to know him.

➢ The therapist can begin to **normalize anxiety** by reviewing that anxiety is a normal reaction and that anxiety problems can be common among kids. The therapist can discuss how many children go the child's school and how likely it is that other children in the child's class have problems with anxiety.

➢ It is important that the therapist **acknowledge, listen to, and respond to the child's concerns** about being in treatment and how the decision was made.

➢ **When resistance or anger is noted**, it may be helpful for the therapist to ask the child "Are there any things that you can think of that would make coming here more fun?" The child can also be given several days to think about being part of treatment. The therapist's position is that she does not want to force the child to change or insist on participation if there are no problems. Instead, the therapist offers herself as someone who might be able to help the child with some things that don't seem to go as well as the child would like.

> **The therapist describes her role to the child as being the child's "coach."** That is, like a coach or a tutor for the child who wants to improve in a skill or learn how to accomplish something that's challenging, the therapist provides structure and helpful hints.

> It is emphasized that **the therapist and child work as a "team"**—the therapist has some suggestions to offer and the child knows himself best.

> **The therapist reviews confidentiality** and the limits of confidentiality with both the parent(s) and child. As a team, the therapist discusses with the parent(s) and child which aspects of the child's treatment and which aspects of the sessions will be shared with the parent(s). Discussing confidentiality during the first session reduces the possibility of a misunderstanding later in treatment.

> To teach different emotions and their somatic responses, the therapist may **use a variety of activities:**

   o **Point to pictures of people showing different expressions** (e.g., from magazines), both facial and entire body, that reflect different emotions and discuss what type of feeling each person might be experiencing (anxious expressions are included but the pictures are not limited to anxiety). Similarly, you can cut the pictures out and create a collage, though this may be too time consuming to do in session. Thus this activity is best left as an optional addition to the child's STIC task for children who appear to be exhibiting difficulty with emotion identification.

   o **Acting out different emotions and their somatic responses (e.g.,** stomachache) as a fun way for the child to learn the session material. Acting silly during role-plays can ease the child's own self-conscious feelings and foster creativity, while setting a nice precedent for future sessions.

   o **Role-playing feelings.** Introduce the idea of role play to the child. Role play with the child, acting out several different types of physically expressed emotions, taking turns guessing the emotion. It can be called "Feelings Charades." The therapist is alert for any difficulties the child is having differentiating and labeling emotions, and spends additional time on this element of the treatment if it is necessary. It is, for example, not uncommon for an anxious child to have trouble differentiating anxious feelings and angry ones or worried feelings and depressive ones.

Parent Session

➢ When explaining the treatment program to the parents, **show the parents a blank _Brief Coping Cat Workbook_** so the parents have a better understanding of the structure of the sessions.

➢ **Set expectations for therapy:** the goal is not the total elimination of anxiety, but the teaching of skills to know how and when to manage anxious arousal.

➢ **The importance of weekly attendance is emphasized** for the parent(s). Parent(s) should be informed that it is important for the child to attend each week to achieve the best treatment results.

➢ **Set expectations about the child's self-disclosure:** parents do not need to report to the therapist every week about things that happened, or be concerned that the child doesn't report them himself. It takes time for the child to feel comfortable. Reminder: inform parents not to grill the child after each session to try to determine what was discussed.

➢ **Address any concerns the parents may feel** uncomfortable about sharing in front of the child.

➢ **Gather information about the parents' understanding of anxiety.** This information helps to assess the extent to which the parents need to be educated about the nature and developmental course of child anxiety.

➢ After talking with the parents, it may be necessary to **teach the parents how to manage their child's anxiety and, if necessary, their own anxiety about the child**. The therapist normalizes the tendency for parents to want to protect or reassure their child or allow their child to avoid distressful situations. However, parents are informed about the "dangers of avoidance" by explaining that, over the long term, avoidance actually maintains anxiety via negative reinforcement. Explain that reinforcing "brave" behavior (through praise, rewards) is preferred. Also explain how parents are models of both "desirable" and "undesirable" behavior. The therapist may also need to address any excessive reassurance behaviors the parents are engaging in.

➤ **A therapist may want to explain "transfer of control:"** effective change involves a gradual transfer of the knowledge, skills, and methods from therapist to child and parent.

➤ It is important that the therapist **point out the strengths of the child** (instead of only talking about the child's anxiety) that may facilitate learning during treatment sessions (e.g., creativity).

Identifying Anxious Feelings, Self-Talk, and Learning to Challenge Thoughts
Session 2

Purpose

Normalize feelings of anxiety. Have the child begin to identify his own specific somatic responses to anxiety. Introduce the "F" Step. Introduce the role of personal thoughts and their impact on response in anxiety-provoking situations. Help the child begin to recognize his self-talk (expectations, automatic questions) in anxious situations. Help the child begin to develop and use coping self-talk.

Goals

1. Review the STIC task from Session 1
2. Discuss and identify the child's specific somatic reactions to anxiety
3. Somatic reactions as cues to increasing anxiety
4. Introduce the "F" step
5. Introduce the concept of thoughts (self-talk)
6. Discuss self-talk in anxiety-provoking situations (anxious self-talk)
7. Differentiate anxious self-talk from coping self-talk
8. Introduce the "E" step
9. Begin to construct a hierarchy of anxiety provoking situations
10. Assign STIC task

Tasks

1. **Review STIC task from Session 1**

   ➢ Discuss the "feeling-great situation" that the child experienced during the intervening days and recorded in the *Brief Coping Cat Workbook*, particularly focusing on the different pleasurable aspects. The therapist asks how the child felt, what the child thought about, and how the child acted. It is unlikely that the child will be able to fully describe such a situation. This limitation, however, can be noted as it may be informative about which aspects of the therapeutic program will need more or less attention and effort. Reward points or give stickers for effort--even modest participation (shaping).

   ➢ If the child did not complete the STIC task from Session 1, the therapist is **not** punitive, but (a) spends time at the start of the session to complete the task and (b) explores why the child was unable to complete the task (e.g., child did not understand assignment, child forgot to complete assignment). The therapist asks the child to think back over the week and to talk about his experiences with the therapist's probing. For any session that the child does not complete the previous week's STIC task, the therapist and child begin by collaborating to complete the STIC task.

   > FLEX

2. **Discuss and identify the child's specific somatic reactions to anxiety**

   ➢ Introduce the variety of somatic feelings that are associated with anxiety including butterflies in the stomach, heart beating fast, flushing of the face, lump in the throat, trembling, etc., by telling a story about people caught in an anxiety-provoking situation and how each one feels during the experience.

   ➢ Ask the child to identify the kinds of somatic responses he has heard about, or that he experienced when in an anxiety-provoking situation. If the child is not able to be specific, suggest that he imagine himself in a safe and neutral situation, imagining how his body feels. The therapist then describes a situation, which is anxiety-provoking for the child, and again asks him to describe how his body feels. Ask the child to describe what his body felt in the anxiety-provoking situation which he did not feel in the safe, neutral situation. This effort is intended to make the somatic signs of anxiety more apparent and clear. Describing the experiences of other people can also help.

3. **Somatic responses as cues to increasing anxiety**
    ➢ Discuss with the child the fact that somatic responses can be a helpful signal that he is becoming anxious and that knowledge of the presence of his anxiety can help him know when to use the coping skills he will learn in later sessions.

    ➢ Provide the child with an example of a time when paying attention to somatic cues can be helpful, such as "A little bit of anxiety before a test helps you remember to study."

4. **Introduce the "F" step**
    ➢ The therapist introduces the child to the idea of a 4-step coping plan, called the FEAR plan. The first step, the "F" step is:
    >   **F**eeling Frightened?
    >   **E**
    >   **A**
    >   **R**

    As part of the "F" step, the child distinguishes anxious feelings, monitors his somatic responses associated with the anxiety, and asks himself, "Am I Feeling frightened?," "How does my body feel?"

5. **Introduce the concept of thoughts (self-talk)**
    ➢ Suggest to the child that now he knows when he becomes anxious, and that there are some thoughts that probably occur along with the feelings.

    ➢ Self-talk in low-stress (concrete) situations FLEX

The therapist describes some fairly concrete and non-stressful, or slightly stressful, situations (e.g., "your pencil falls on the floor" or "your mother is serving broccoli for dinner and you hate broccoli"). The child is asked to give some samples of thoughts that would accompany these events (i.e., "What would be in your bubble?"). The child thinks of a situation and describes what thoughts might occur to someone else who just experienced that situation.

6. **Discuss self-talk in anxiety-provoking situations (anxious self-talk)**

   ➢ Using situations from the child's hierarchy, the therapist and child work together to identify common themes in the child's own anxious self-talk. The therapist makes a connection between the thought "something bad is going to happen" and anxious feelings.

7. **Differentiate anxious self-talk from coping self-talk**

   ➢ Using situations from the child's hierarchy, the therapist and child work together to identify coping self-talk the child could use to challenge the child's own anxious self-talk. Ask the child to help think of thoughts that (a) would lead him to experience more distress (i.e., anxious self-talk) and (b) would help him to reduce distress (i.e., coping self-talk). The therapist introduces the idea of coping self-talk, or thoughts that help people reduce distress in anxious situations. The therapist and child discuss how the child might change his behavior depending on the way he thought about what had happened. Examples of coping thoughts include: "I can do this", "It'll be hard, but I can get through it", "I have done this before I can do it again", "I probably won't be hurt". Note: Children often suggest thoughts that are unrealistic to carry out as the child does not believe them, such as "I shouldn't worry" or "I won't get hurt". The therapist should take care to help the child generate thoughts that are helpful in the feared situation.

8. **Introduce the "E" Step**

   ➢ Introduces the child to the second step, or the "E" step:

   Feeling Frightened?

Expecting bad things to happen?

A

R

Explain that as part of the "E" step, the child monitors his thoughts associated with anxiety and asks himself, "What is my self-talk?" "What am I expecting to happen?" Illustrate how if someone is thinking negative thoughts, the person can then attempt to reduce his distress through changing the self-talk to coping self-talk.

9. **Begin to construct a hierarchy of anxiety-provoking situations**

   ➤ Begin to construct a hierarchy. Begin to discuss the specifics of the child's anxieties, including the types of situations that provoke anxiety, the child's reactions to anxiety (somatic and cognitive), and the child's response in the anxiety-provoking situations. Make sure to identify the child's anxious self-talk about each anxiety provoking situation.

   ➤ If the child finds it difficult to be specific about his anxieties, the therapist can use a procedure, recommended by Ollendick and Cerny (1981), in which the child tries to imagine an actual situation while the therapist observes his behavior for signs of anxiety. To introduce the procedure, the therapist models the process by imagining herself in an anxiety-provoking situation while describing each step. The child can then be invited to tag-along as the therapist repeats the imagining process with another situation and, finally, to imagine himself in an anxiety-provoking situation—with the therapist providing prompts as needed. Although the therapist can be encouraging by use of sights, sounds, and pictures, children will differ in their response to the use of imaginal exposure.

   ➤ From the data collected thus far, the therapist and child begin to construct a brief hierarchy of the situations that seem to provoke anxiety in the child. The therapist guides the child to use situations that may be practiced when constructing the hierarchy. For example, a child with performance anxiety could be asked to read a poem to the therapist. In order to adequately design an exposure task, it is essential to ascertain the child's **feared outcome** in each situation. For example, designing an exposure task for a child who is anxious at school because he is afraid he will have to answer a question in class will involve the child actually being asked a question and using the FEAR steps to cope with the experience. In this case, just practicing going to school will not allow the child to face the real situation. It is important to be as specific as possible when designing a hierarchy (see a list of exposure task suggestions in Kendall et al., 2005a or Kendall & Khanna, 2008).

➤ To record this information, the therapist and child use either the situation cards found on pages 53-54 of the *Brief Coping Cat Workbook* or the "fear ladder" found on page 55 of the *Brief Coping Cat Workbook*. The decision as to which method to use can be made collaboratively. For young children, categorizing fears into "easy," "medium," and "challenging" may be a more simplistic and understandable procedure than building an actual hierarchy using the fear ladder. Regardless of the method chosen to document the child's fears (situation cards or fear ladder), the therapist takes note of which aspects of the different situations seem to be particularly easy and troublesome for the child. Be as specific as possible regarding the situations. Vague language is not preferred (e.g., "going to school"). Instead, enter specific situations such as "taking a math test at school" or "eating in the cafeteria." Encourage the child to add to the cards/ladder whenever he remembers situations in which he feels anxious.

10. <u>Assign STIC task</u>

➤ Remind the child about the STIC task and review the idea of using the *Brief Coping Cat Workbook* he was given in Session 1 as a journal to record his experiences. Or, if needed, the events can be digitally recorded. This method allows for more immediate recording.

➤ For the following session, ask the child to record in his *Brief Coping Cat Workbook* one anxious experience and one non-anxious experience, describing what happened, how the child knew he was anxious, how he felt, and what he thought.

➢ Ask the child to write down what happened as precisely as possible and to add any additional information he wishes. Ask the child to enter information into his workbook as soon as possible after the experience, when it is fresh.

➢ If appropriate, the therapist models recording a STIC situation for the child. The therapist imagines herself in an anxiety-provoking situation and writing a description of the imagined experience. The therapist asks the child to imagine himself in a situation as the therapist describes it and records the event in the way he will be recording his actual experiences.

➢ Take a few minutes to engage in a fun activity at the end of the session.

Tips from the Trenches

Session 2

➤ All **concepts can be introduced by first referring to other people** rather than focusing on the child's own feelings or experiences. For example, the therapist can discuss how the child knows what friends or family members are feeling based on their facial expressions and body postures. Begin with people who are familiar to the child without having to focus immediately on the child's own specific concerns.

➤ Sometimes the therapist may notice distress in the child even when the therapist is only role-playing her own experiences with anxiety. These children tend to have difficulty differentiating their own emotional experience from the experiences of others around them. In such cases, **proceed slowly toward independent role play using the "tag-along" procedure.**

➤ The therapist can **talk about how animals show their fear**, for example, how a cat's hair stands on end or how a dog puts his tail between his legs. Mentioning that even animals sometimes get nervous or scared helps to normalize anxiety.

➤ To teach different emotions and their somatic responses, the therapist may **use a variety of activities:**

  • **Engage in a "body drawing" activity.** On a large piece of butcher paper, the therapist and child draw an outline of a body or trace the child's body. The body is then "filled in" by drawing the various physical symptoms of anxiety that people experience (e.g., pounding heart, sweaty palms, lump in throat, etc.) The child and therapist take turns circling or labeling the physical symptoms that are specific to each person.

  • **The therapist and child can play a guessing game** to make learning about somatic responses more fun. The therapist and child can take turns guessing what emotion the other is feeling when their body reacts a certain way (acted out).

➤ **The therapist can use the "fire alarm" analogy to help explain the experience of somatic responses**. Physical symptoms warn us when there is danger. Sometimes, though, the alarm will go off when there is no emergency

31

(false alarms) because the alarm system has malfunctioned, or is turned up too much. In these cases, the therapist will help the child to learn to "send back the fire trucks" because there is no danger. Keep it fun.

> **The anxiety rating scale can be a fire alarm indicator.** When it reaches a certain level, the alarm sounds: when you reach a certain level, that's when you know that it is time to do something or ask for help. This analogy gives the child a rationale for why we are paying attention to feelings.

> The thought-bubble activity may help the child understand the concept of self-talk if they are having difficulty grasping the concept- show cartoons with empty bubbles (see pp. 9-12 in the *Brief Coping Cat Workbook*). Together with the therapist, the child fills in the possible thoughts for different cartoons. The cartoons portray fairly simple scenes in which the character's thoughts are likely to be fairly obvious and include a number of different types of feelings.

> To help the child identify his anxious self-talk, the **therapist can ask the child to draw a picture of himself in an anxious situation and then draw thought bubbles over the pictures** that can be filled in. This activity may be especially useful for artistic/creative children or children who tend to have difficulty verbalizing their thoughts and/or emotions.

> For older children, it may be useful to illustrate the idea of self-talk by **providing examples of television shows in which the main character is the narrator** (e.g., Lizzie Maguire, the Wonder Years, Scrubs, etc.)

> The **therapist checks with the child about whether he believes his coping thoughts**, because the child may be able to think of alternatives but not believe they are valid. A child may need to be encouraged to generate thoughts that are non-distressing and relevant to the particular situation, and to be assisted in seeing their true merits.

> Children can also **identify imaginary or real people whom they admire as "good at coping"** and use them as models. At times, if the client cannot generate coping thoughts, or is unwilling to consider other possibilities, he can think about how the hero or "good coper" might think differently.

> Caution: **Be careful not to fall in the trap of trying to convince the child that a scary event is not going to happen**. A good strategy is for the therapist and child to reverse roles—have the child "act" the part of the coach or detective and

try to convince the therapist that a situation is unlikely to happen. It is also helpful to discuss with the child what might be done if his worst possible fear ever does come true.

➢ Discuss thinking traps

Encourage the child to be a detective and look for thinking traps that can trick people into feeling anxious before they have had a chance to collect evidence. Due to the brief nature of this treatment it is not advised that the therapist discuss all thinking traps with the child. Rather it is suggested that the therapist identify and label thinking traps they notice the child engaging in if/when it happens in session.

- **Walking with blinders**
  Only seeing the negative and overlooking the good in a situation
  [Race horses wear "blinders" to see straight and not be distracted in a race]
- **The repetitor**
  If it happened once it is always going to happen that way
- **The catastrophiser (or the pessimist)**
  Always thinking the 'worst ever' is going to happen
- **The avoider**
  Staying away from situations you think are scary without trying first
- **The mind reader (or fortune-teller, using the "crystal ball")**
  Jumping to conclusions about a person/thing/situation without the facts
- **The shoulds**
  I SHOULD always be perfect. I SHOULDN'T make mistakes.
- **The perfectionist**
  Setting expectations that are too high: Perfection is not a human option.

➢ The therapist and child can **make a list of thinking traps** (renaming them to fit) typically used by the child himself. When apt, the child can take the list home and post it on the refrigerator so that he is reminded of the potential "traps."

➢ When beginning to build the fear hierarchy, **it is helpful for the therapist to have an idea in advance of the situations the child may want to put on the hierarchy** (usually gathered at an initial or intake assessment). If the child is having difficulty thinking of situations to put on the hierarchy, the therapist can mention some ideas specific to the child by suggesting that "other kids I work with have been anxious about ____, is that something you would like to work on too?"

➢ Some children may over- or under-report their anxiety. Remember that items placed on the hierarchy can be reevaluated to ensure their appropriately and accurately represent the child's anxieties.

Introducing Problem Solving, Self-Evaluation, and Self-Reward
Session 3

Purpose

Introduce the role of personal thoughts and their impact on response in anxiety-provoking situations. Help the child begin to recognize his self-talk (e.g., expectations, automatic questions) in anxious situations. Help the child begin to develop and use coping self-talk. Introduce the concept of problem-solving and develop and use problem-solving strategies to better manage anxiety. Introduce the concept of evaluating or rating performance and rewarding yourself for effort.

Goals

1. Review STIC task from Session 2
2. Introduce the "A" and "R" steps
3. Introduce the concept of problem solving
4. Practice coping self-talk and problem solving in anxious situations
5. Continue to construct a hierarchy of anxious symptoms
6. Assign STIC task

Tasks

1. **Review STIC task from Session 2**

> ➢ Encourage the child to share the experiences he recorded. Focus the discussion on the somatic feelings that he experienced during these episodes. Reward with stickers or points for STIC task completion. If the STIC was not completed, do it with the child at the start of the session.

> ➢ Discuss the child's experiences when practicing relaxing, noting the parts that went well and those that did not. Initiate a discussion with the child about his experiences recording the anxiety-provoking situations during the intervening days. Focus on anxious and non-anxious somatic feelings (to reinforce the skills from Sessions 2 and 3). Listen for any suggestion from the child of thoughts or expectations associated with these experiences and, in age-appropriate terms, call them to his attention. Reward the child with 2 points as appropriate. If the STIC was not completed, do it with the child at the start of the session.

2. **Introduce the "A" and "R" Steps**

> ➢ The therapist introduces the child to the third step to coping with anxiety in the FEAR plan, the "A" step:

>> **F**eeling Frightened?

>> **E**xpecting bad things to happen?

>> **A**ttitudes and actions that can help

>> **R**

> The therapist explains to the child that in addition to recognizing his anxious feelings and self-talk, he may find it helpful to take some action that will help change the situation so he can proceed despite his anxiety.

> ➢ The therapist introduces the child to the fourth step to coping with anxiety in the FEAR plan, the "R" step:

>> **F**eeling Frightened?

>> **E**xpecting bad things to happen?

Attitudes and actions that can help

Results and rewards

➢ The therapist describes a reward as something that is given when you're pleased with the work that was gone. Introduce the idea of rating his performance and rewarding himself for efforts to cope and to stay in a situation despite his anxiety. Be sure to point out that it is not reasonable to expect to succeed every time he tries something new, and not always succeeding is not a problem. All that is asked is that one tries his best.

➢ The therapist and the child collaborate to come up with a list of rewards for the child. Discuss with the child appropriate reward sizes (not too big), point out that rewards work best when they are immediate, and encourage a mix of material (e.g., trading cards) and nonmaterial (reading a book; computer time) rewards. Introduce the idea of social reward, such as going to a movie with friends or playing a game with someone. Potential rewards are entered into the "reward menu" on p. 52 of the workbook.

6. **Introduce the concept of problem solving**

➢ Describe the problem-solving process.

The therapist explains that problem solving helps to develop a plan for coping with anxiety. This plan will be specific to the type of situation and the child's particular preference for strategies that are helpful to him. Discuss problem solving by describing for the child how to develop an idea for changing something, using the following steps:

FLEX

Step 1
✦ Define the problem:
What is the anxious situation?

Step 2
✦ Explore potential alternative solutions (be careful not to evaluate yet!):
What might someone do to make this situation less fearful?

Step 3

➔ Evaluate the potential alternative solutions:
   Which solutions are feasible alternatives?
   Do any alternative solutions NOT make sense or are any NOT feasible?

Step 4

➔ Select the preferred alternative:
   What might be one of the best things to do?
   What is the preferred solution?

➢ This presentation will have to be modified to accommodate the child's developmental level, particularly in terms of the language and cognitive ability. Some children will be able to understand and comprehend the ideas as presented, but the language level will have to be lowered. For young children, the procedure may simply have to be taught by example and practice. Limit your explanation to a brief overview (approximately 5 minutes), as you will review problem solving with the child in more detail when reviewing the FEAR plan in following sessions.

➢ Provide examples of times when problem solving could be useful.

7. **Practicing using the FEAR plan in an anxious situation.**

➢ Practice using the FEAR plan

The therapist models, and the child tags along, practicing the "F", "E", "A", and "R" steps and monitoring thoughts in increasing anxiety-provoking situations, going through the following questions:

Feeling frightened?

➔ Ask myself:
   Am I feeling anxious? What's happening in my body?

Expecting bad things to happen?

➔ Ask myself:
   What is my self-talk? What am I expecting to happen?
➔ Gather evidence for the thought (be like a detective or scientist!):

Do I know for sure this is going to happen? What else might happen? What has happened before? Has this happened to anyone I know? How many times has it happened before?

✦ Having collected all the evidence:
How likely is it to happen? What is a coping thought I can have in this situation? What is the worst thing that could happen? What would be so bad about that?

| What are the **A**ctions or **A**ttitudes that might help? |

✦ Begin Problem Solving!

| Results and Rewards |

✦ How did I do? What did I learn?
✦ How will I reward myself for my bravery?

8. **Continue to construct a hierarchy of anxiety-provoking situations (limit to 5-10 minutes)**

➢ The therapist reviews with the child the items already added to his hierarchy and works with the child to identify additional situations to add.

9. **Assign STIC task**

➢ During the next week, the child is asked to record in the *Brief Coping Cat Workbook* two situations in which he felt anxious and pay special attention to his thoughts and actions.

➢ If time allows, at the end of the session, take a few minutes to play a game or engage in a fun activity.

Tips from the Trenches

Session 3

➢ **Make a "coping card."** Encourage the child to make a card of potential coping thoughts and/or "detective" questions to take with him into anxiety-provoking situations. For younger children, a card with an image to represent their coping thought may also be useful.

➢ Keep in mind that the **brainstorming part of problem-solving is done without evaluative comment.** The merits of the various options are not examined until after the list is done—we don't want to inhibit the child nor discredit a good idea before giving it a chance.

➢ It's a **good idea for the therapist to have some suggestions in mind when considering alternative solutions**. Here are a few: try to change the situation (instrumental coping); yell or cry (emotional intervention); distraction (think about something else); think differently (coping thoughts); seek emotional support (family, friends); do nothing. Give some funny or silly solutions too!

➢ To **integrate information**, the therapist can choose a few thought bubble pictures that demonstrate potentially anxiety-provoking situations (e.g., a girl dropping her lunch tray) and the child and therapist can attempt to recall the "thoughts," challenge those thoughts, generate coping thoughts, and problem solve about how to make the situation less-anxiety-provoking for the child in the picture. Remember that it is easier for the child to practice when talking about someone else (child in the cartoon).

Reviewing Skills Already Learned, Practicing in Low Anxiety-Provoking Situations, and the Second Parent Meeting (Exposure Tasks)
Session 4

Purpose

Finalize hierarchy of anxious symptoms. Review and apply the 4-step FEAR plan. Begin practicing and applying the skills for coping with anxiety in situations that produce low levels of anxiety for the child. Encourage continued parental cooperation in the treatment program. Answer parents' questions and address parental concerns.

Goals

Child session (60 minutes)

1. Review STIC task from Session 3
2. Finalize construction of a hierarchy of anxious symptoms
3. Review the idea of progressing from learning new skills to practicing new skills
4. Review and apply the FEAR plan to a low anxiety-provoking situation
5. Begin practicing using exposure in low anxiety-provoking situation
6. Plan exposure task(s) for Session 5
7. Acknowledge upcoming parent session
8. Assign STIC task

Parent session (30 minutes)

1. Provide information about the second half of treatment (i.e., exposure tasks)
2. Provide parents an opportunity to ask questions and discuss their concerns (time-limited).
3. Learn more about the situations in which the child becomes anxious
4. Offer specific ways the parents can be involved in the second half of treatment

Tasks (Child Session)

1. **Review STIC task from Session 3**

> ➤ Discuss with the child the anxious experiences he described in his *Brief Coping Cat Workbook*. Focus the discussion on how the child knew he was anxious and what his anxious self-talk was. Have the child describe his experience developing a plan of action when faced with an anxious situation--be sure to encourage and support even partial successes. Remind the child that mastering these skills requires lots of practice. Reward the child for effort and cooperation with two points or stickers, as appropriate. If the STIC was not completed, do it with the child at the start of the session.

> ➤ Discuss the child's experiences during the week practicing relaxation, noting both the times that went well and those in which he experienced difficulty. Discuss the child's experiences using relaxation as a first response when becoming anxious.

2. **Finalize construction of a hierarchy of anxiety-provoking situations**

> ➤ The therapist and child review the child's fear hierarchy and work together to identify additional situations to add. The working version of the hierarchy is agreed upon.

3. **Review the idea of progressing from learning new skills to practicing new skills**

> ➤ The therapist informs the child that the next step in treatment involves practicing the skills that have been learned. "We'll go places and do things." The following information may need to be discussed with the child:

> > ✦ **The FEAR steps will be practiced in situations in which the child feels anxious or worried** (i.e., the situations identified on the situation cards (pp. 53-54) and/or fear ladder (p. 55) in the *Brief Coping Cat Workbook*). Practicing these steps in situations that provoke genuine anxiety allows the child to see that he can cope and to find out that what he thought was going to happen in the situation is unlikely to happen.

41

- **The practice will be carried out in a gradual way.** The child will start practicing in situations that make him only a little anxious (i.e. the Easy situation cards/bottom of fear ladder). Step by step we'll move up to approach some tougher situations (i.e. the Medium and Challenging situation cards/higher entries on the fear ladder). Once the child builds some confidence, we can try even tougher situations.

- **The aim of the treatment is not to remove the child's anxiety** all together but to reduce it to a normal level and to be able to manage it. It's like turning down a radio volume from a high volume of 10 to a normal volume of 2—the radio is still on, the volume is just lowered.

- **The child will experience some anxiety when practicing his skills,** but this is to be expected and is OK. *The more he practices facing these situations the less anxious he will feel,* and the more his mastery and confidence will build.

- **The fear steps need to be practiced repeatedly.** Facing situations that make the child feel anxious will be practiced over and over again. Practice will take place almost until the child feels bored with the situation rather than anxious. The practice is done both in and out of session.

- **Depending on the exposure task, the child may need to stay in the situation for a certain duration of time.** The aim of an exposure task is for the child to realize that he can cope with the situation and that what he thought was going to happen is not likely to happen. If he gets out of the situation too quickly, then he hasn't experienced that he can cope and the next time he enters the situation he will feel the same or even more anxiety.

➢ The therapist and child plan the first exposure task for later this session, choosing something from the 'easy' cards or at the bottom of the fear ladder.

4. **Review and apply the FEAR plan**

➢ The FEAR acronym makes recall of the steps easier and facilitates successful coping. Children are encouraged to use the FEAR acronym during the sessions. If the child wants to be more creative, or has difficulty with the FEAR acronym, encourage him to generate his own acronym to remember the steps. To prepare for the first exposure session and ensure adequate understanding of the FEAR plan, the therapist and child develop a FEAR plan for coping with the session 4 exposure task and enter it in the *Brief Coping*

FLEX

Cat Workbook (p. 19). Anticipate the child's negative thinking and avoidance behavior, and have in place a plan to engage in the situation despite any hesitancy. The therapist and child negotiate a reward to be given after the child completes the exposure. If the child has difficulty with any of the steps, take time to review. Note that some children may ask lots of questions or want to spend time reviewing in an effort to avoid the exposure task. Therefore, it is important to limit the time spent on review - it is very important that the child go through with the exposure task!

5. **Begin practicing using exposure in low anxiety-provoking situation**

For each exposure task practiced:

➢ Preparation | FLEX |

Review the first practice situation chosen by the therapist and the child. To prepare, the therapist and child review the previously developed FEAR plan for the upcoming anxious situation located in the *Brief Coping Cat Workbook* (p. 23). Be sure you have anticipated the child's anxious thinking and avoidance behavior, and have in place a plan to engage in the situation despite any hesitancy. The therapist and child negotiate a reward to be given after the child completes the exposure.

If possible, the therapist then sets up props to create a scene and asks the child to role play the situation as he goes through the FEAR plan. For example, if the task will involve initiating a conversation with a small group of people who are sitting together, then the "props" for the situation, in addition to 3 or 4 colleagues who will role-play being kids in the school cafeteria, include lunch trays, food, and perhaps a lunch bell.

| FLEX |

➢ Practice

Ask the child to actually practice the situation that he has role played and to note any difficulties with use of the FEAR steps. The therapist then encourages positive self-rating and self-reward for partial success and helps with any portion of the exercise where the child experienced difficulty. If required, the child repeats the exercise, using the FEAR plan without the therapist's help.

Throughout the exposure task, the child provides a SUDS rating every minute and then again at the completion of the practice. The therapist also provides her own SUDS ratings of how anxious she feels the child is at pre-, during (every minute), and post-exposure.

Following the exposure task the child is rewarded for effort. Help the child to process and make sense of the experience after it is completed: for example, discuss what the child found easiest and most difficult and develop ideas for further improvement.

Discuss what the child learned during the exposure task. What did he learn about: his anxiety, staying in the situation, not avoiding, the situation itself, his coping strategies, what he might do next time.

Depending on the ability level of the child and the time available during session, more than one exposure task may be completed during session.

6. **Plan exposure task(s) for Session 5**
   ➢ Using the situation cards/fear ladder in the *Brief Coping Cat Workbook* (pp. 53-54), collaborate with the child and decide on the situation that will be practiced in Session 5. The situation is associated with moderate levels of anxiety. Mention that next week the child will be practicing his coping skills using the FEAR plan in more challenging situations and maintain a positive, adventurous outlook.

7. **Acknowledge upcoming parent meeting**
   ➢ Remind the child that the next part of the session will be held with his parent(s). It is okay to reassure the child that the therapist will not share personal information during the parent session. For example, the therapist can ask "Is there anything you don't want me to talk about when I meet

with your parent(s)"? The therapist informs the child that she is interested in what his parents have to say and how they can be of help.

8.   **Assign STIC task**

➢ Ask the child to practice using the FEAR steps in three anxious situations that provoke mild anxiety and to record in his workbook what happened for discussion during the next session. When choosing practice exposure tasks, it is recommended to choose no more than one task that is expected to be time consuming for the child to do or for the parents to help arrange. Collaborate on a reward for the STIC tasks.

➢ The child is also asked to explain the FEAR acronym to a parent, using the FEAR plan ID if needed. This experience helps the child understand the coping plan and also provides the parents with an understanding of the plan.

➢ At the end of the session, before meeting with the parent(s), take a few minutes to play a game or engage in a fun activity if time permits.

Tasks (Parent Session)

1. **<u>Provide additional information about the second half of treatment (i.e., exposure tasks)</u>**

   ➢ Provide a brief outline of the remainder of the treatment program (refer to the *Parent Companion* as needed) and briefly explain the features of the second half of treatment. Explain that the child will be practicing the skills that he has learned. As presented to the child during the child session portion during today's session, the following information also may need to be presented to the parents (see child session for additional details):

   - **The FEAR steps will be practiced in situations in which the child feels anxious or worried.**

   - **The practice will be carried out in a gradual way.**

   - **The aim of the treatment is not to remove the child's anxiety but to reduce their anxiety so that it is at the level of most other children the child's age.**

   - **The child will experience some anxiety when practicing his skills.**

   - **The fear steps need to be practiced repeatedly.**

   - **Depending on the exposure task, the child may need to stay in the situation for a certain duration of time.**

   ➢ After explaining the rationale behind the use of exposure tasks, the therapist acknowledges that this portion of the treatment will invoke some anxiety for the child before a reduction in anxiety is observed (i.e., anxiety goes up a bit before it comes way down). Spend time with the parents normalizing this process for them. Solicit the parent's help in refining the child's hierarchy, especially when the children are young or appear to have difficulty providing accurate ratings.

2. **<u>Provide parents an opportunity to ask questions and discuss their concerns</u>**

   ➢ The therapist invites the parents to discuss their concerns about the child or about the child's participation in the second half of treatment, particularly the exposure tasks. With open-ended questions, invite the parents to provide any additional history or current information which they feel will be helpful in understanding the child and constructing useful exposure tasks. Keep this part of the session time limited (e.g, 10 minutes or less).

3.   **<u>Learn more about the situations in which the child becomes anxious</u>**

➢ Using what has been learned to date, talk generally about (a) impressions of situations that are troublesome for the child and (b) the child's typical somatic and cognitive responses to anxiety. Invite the parents to share their impressions and provide examples of situations in which they believe the child feels anxious and needs practice.

4.   **<u>Offer specific ways the parents can be involved in the second half of treatment</u>**

➢ Invite the parents to assist in the execution of an exposure tasks, in session and at home, when appropriate/necessary. The parents are invited to call the therapist if they have additional helpful information or if they have further questions. Depending on the age of the child and the quality of parental support, the therapist may ask for the parents' help in other specific areas related to the child during the coming weeks.

Tips from the Trenches

Child Session

➢ Anxious children set high standards and rarely reward themselves for their accomplishments and, instead, tend to rely on outside sources for this sense of achievement. **Encourage the child to feel proud of his efforts and his accomplishments** and ask the child to describe for you a situation in which he felt proud of himself. Note to the child how someone (e.g., TV star) felt proud because he did something challenging.

➢ The therapist encourages the child to pick a favorite activity for both the child and therapist to do together following the session to **reward the child for his effort thus far.** Social rewards are terrific "together time." Be certain to allow time for the reward, and follow through on the plan.

➢ **Encourage the child to reward himself with positive self-statements** such as "I did a great job," or "I did it!" It may also be useful for the child to reward himself in situations where he is unable to provide himself with a material reward by imagining a pleasant event or scene. For example, when a child faces a stressful situation in school he can reward himself by imagining himself jumping up and down or doing a victory dance (e.g., a "touchdown" dance).

➢ **Create a "FEAR Plan ID"**—a pocket/wallet-sized index card such as the one on p. 56 of the workbook. The first letter of each FEAR step is emphasized in some colorful way. The child decorates the card creatively and personalizes the card with coping thoughts, possible rewards, etc. The therapist provides the crayons, markers, and stickers, laminates the card, and gives the child the card to carry with him.

➢ With a younger client, it is helpful to have him **explain the 4-step coping plan to his parent(s)** in front of the therapist so that the therapist can assist if needed. For older children, it is suggested that the child talk to his parent(s) about the steps independently unless he wants the therapist there.

- **Stories about an imaginary group of kids in a stressful situation may be particularly helpful** with younger or lower functioning children who may have difficulty describing/generating situations in which they feel anxious.

- Note for the child how **imagining how to handle a situation (an imaginal exposure task) is helpful for beginning to use various coping strategies**. Practice helps in the actual situation.

- If the child is extremely anxious, **the therapist may begin with imaginal exposure tasks until the child's level of anxiety is reduced** and the child is able to demonstrate use of the coping plan.

- The therapist may **model an exposure task** for the child while having the child record the therapist's SUDS ratings. This may be especially useful for children who appear to be having difficulty providing accurate SUDS ratings for themselves.

- **Be prepared, and be confident.** That is, know what features of the situation are distressing and have ideas in mind for addressing them. Be encouraging and supportive, and exude confidence: it's amazing how youth will "give it a go" with the right preparation. Your style will influence the child's willingness to be involved. The exposure tasks are never punitive.

- When preparing to complete an exposure task, be sure to ask the child about aspects of the situation that are likely to be troublesome so that the therapist and child can **problem-solve ways to cope with the potential difficulties prior to the exposure task.**

- The child's involvement is critical. **Increase involvement by soliciting the child's suggestions** in planning the exposure tasks. The therapist can toss out ideas, but include the child's opinions on how to make the exposure especially useful. The child's suggestions are evidence of involvement and are welcomed.

- **The fear hierarchy (situation cards/fear ladder) may need to be changed or amended throughout the exposure sessions** to reflect changes in the level of fear in the child-reported situations. Some degree of adjustment is expected. However, be cautious not to accept the child's self report (e.g., "Oh, that situation isn't stressful for me any more") that the hierarchy needs to be changed. Instead, test out the situation with the child as an "experiment", in a nonconfrontive fashion.

- **Do not be drawn to "protect" the child** from negative emotions. One of the features of *in-vivo* exposure is for the therapist to <u>allow</u> the child to become anxious. Any natural tendency to reassure, comfort, "save," or protect the child is held back so the child can begin to develop/display independent skills for coping. Children may try to avoid the *in-vivo* experience by engaging the therapist in talking excessively about the situation and all its difficulties. The concerns are addressed, but the child, nevertheless, approaches the situation.

- Note: **do not "battle" with the child about an exposure task.** If the child is resistant, be patient. Also, the therapist can work with the child to modify the current exposure task a bit or generate an alternative. Although some negotiation is acceptable, it is important for the therapist not to allow the child to avoid genuine experience with and practicing in the feared situation.

- During exposure tasks, the therapist needs to **be aware of "subtle avoidance"** behavior. Subtle avoidance behavior during an exposure task will not allow the child to face the situations "full on." For example, the socially anxious child may be imaging and practicing "going to a school activity," but when he gets to the activity he may stand by himself, not talking to anyone. The preferred experience would include engaging in a conversation. Another example could be the separation anxious child who brings a special object into an anxiety-provoking situation to make the situation feel safe (e.g., mother's car keys), or the anxious child who uses distraction to think of something completely different when in the anxiety-provoking situation. Although all of these behaviors allow the child to face the situation, in a way the child is prevented from facing the situation full on. It is okay for the child to use a behavior such as these as a coping strategy to begin with (because this is a step by step process), but eventually it is preferred that the child face the situation without any crutches.

- **Various *in-vivo* experiences can be arranged in the office:** setting up testing situations, having the child give a speech or read a poem in front of a small audience, using a video camera to videotape the child, and/or having the child introduce himself to other office personnel.

- **Many natural-occurring exposure tasks can occur in public places** (e.g., malls, arcades, churches, restaurants, playgrounds, etc.) or in academic and social situations arranged in schools with the help of teachers and guidance counselors.

The use of naturally occurring exposure tasks is encouraged because of their less-contrived, true to life nature.

➢ **Other exposure experiences are planned within the office, but carried out with parental help as they naturally occur** (e.g., going to a party or inviting a friend over a child's house). Parental involvement allows the therapist greater flexibility in planning, but this depends on the parents' abilities and motivation. Such situations as family trips, separations, or band/play/sports team tryouts are naturally occurring opportunities that can be used.

➢ **The therapist can take pictures of the child during the exposure.** These pictures can be used for "bragging rights" (i.e., to show others the child's bravery).

➢ **SUDS ratings taken during the exposure situation can have multiple uses:**

　✦ SUDS ratings can provide feedback to the child about the level of anxiety in the context of the feared object/situation.

　✦ SUDS ratings can be viewed and treated as "data" regarding what happens to the youth's anxiety when in a specific situation. The child and therapist can graph the data and discuss the SUDS ratings (e.g., Did the anxiety ratings go down at all? Did the ratings go up first before they went down? Do the ratings for each exposure task follow a pattern?).

　✦ SUDS ratings can be used to determine the exposure task length. To maximize beneficial gains, most exposure tasks call for children to remain in contact with the feared stimulus or in the provocative situation until SUDS are reduced by at least 50 percent.

　✦ A visual analogue scale, such as a "Feelings Thermometer" presented in Session 1, can be a helpful way to explain SUDS ratings to children. Most children are familiar with how a thermometer works. Just like a regular thermometer, the SUDS thermometer measures distress such that the higher the "mercury," the greater the distress.

Parent Session

➢ Review negative reinforcement, avoidance, and reassurance seeking with parents. Check in with parents to see how they are doing with modifying these behaviors.

Practicing in Moderately Anxiety-Provoking Situations
(Exposure Tasks)
Session 5

Purpose

Begin practicing and applying the skills for coping with anxiety in situations that produce moderate levels of anxiety for the child.

Goals

1. Review STIC task from Session 4
2. Practice using exposure in moderately anxiety-provoking situation(s)
3. Plan exposure task(s) for Session 6
4. Assign STIC task

Tasks

1. **Review STIC task from Session 4**

   ➤ Initiate a discussion about the intervening days with respect to the child's anxiety—how he's improving in terms of coping and managing it and how he's rewarding himself for his progress. Discuss the two situations recorded in his *Brief Coping Cat Workbook*, focusing particularly on the child's experiences with recalling and using the FEAR plan. Address any difficulties with the four steps. Be encouraging: with practice, the four steps will be almost automatic and not require as much concentration as they do in the beginning.

   ➤ Ask the child to describe his experiences when explaining the 4-step plan to a parent. Reward the child for his cooperation with points, as appropriate. If any part of the STIC was not completed, do it with the child at the start of the session.

   ➤ Reward the child's cooperation with points/stickers as appropriate. If any part of the STIC was not completed, do it with the child at the start of the session or practice the anxious experience planned for the STIC during today's session if possible.

2. **Practice using exposure in moderately anxiety-provoking situation(s)**
   For each exposure task practiced:
   ➤ Preparation   FLEX

   Review the practice situation chosen by the therapist and the child in Session 4. To prepare, the therapist and child review the previously developed FEAR plan for the upcoming anxious situation located in the *Brief Coping Cat Workbook* (p. 30). Be sure you have anticipated the child's anxious thinking and avoidance behavior, and have in place a plan to engage in the situation despite any hesitancy. The therapist and child negotiate a reward to be given after the child completes the exposure.

The therapist then sets up props to create a scene and asks the child to role play the situation as he goes through the FEAR plan. For example, if the task will involve initiating a conversation with a small group of people who are sitting together, then the "props" for the situation, in addition to 3 or 4 colleagues who will role-play being kids in the school cafeteria, include lunch trays, food, and perhaps a lunch bell.

➤ Practice

Ask the child to actually practice the situation that he has role played and to note any difficulties with use of the FEAR steps. The therapist then encourages positive self-rating and self-reward for partial success and helps with any portion of the exercise where the child experienced difficulty. If required, the child repeats the exercise, using the FEAR plan without the therapist's help.

Throughout the exposure task, the child provides a SUDS rating every minute and then again at the completion of the practice. The therapist also provides her own SUDS ratings of how anxious she feels the child is at pre-, during (every minute), and post-exposure.

Following the exposure task the child is rewarded. Help the child to process and make sense of the experience after it is completed: discuss what the child found easiest and most difficult and develop ideas for further improvement.

Discuss what the child learned during the exposure task. What did he learn about: his anxiety, staying in the situation, not avoiding, the situation itself, his coping strategies, what he might do next time.

Depending on the ability level of the child and the time available during session, more than one exposure task may be completed during session.

3. **Plan exposure task(s) for Session 6**

   ➤ Using the situation cards/fear ladder in the *Brief Coping Cat Workbook* (pp. 53-54), collaborate with the child and decide on the situation that will be practiced in Session 6. The situation is associated with high levels of anxiety. Mention that next week the child will be practicing his coping skills using the FEAR plan in more challenging situations and maintain a positive, adventurous outlook.

4. **Assign STIC task**

   ➤ Ask the child to practice using the FEAR steps in three anxious situations that provoke mild anxiety and to record in his workbook what happened for discussion during the next session. When choosing practice exposure tasks, it is recommended to choose no more than one task that is expected to be time consuming for the child to do or for the parents to help arrange. Collaborate on a reward for the STIC tasks. The child is also asked to cut out a picture from a magazine or draw a picture of a cartoon character (or sci-fi character) who can help him cope when he is feeling anxious and to bring his character to the next session.

   ➤ Take a few minutes to play a game or engage in a fun activity at the end of the session as a reward for the child's participation in his first practice session.

Practicing in High Anxiety-Provoking Situations (Exposure Tasks)
Session 6

Purpose

Practice applying the skills for coping with anxiety in imaginal and *in-vivo* situations that produce high levels of anxiety in the child.

Goals

1. Review STIC task from Session 5
2. Practice using exposure in high anxiety-provoking situations
3. Plan exposure task(s) for Session 7
4. Assign STIC task

Tasks

1. **Review STIC task from Session 5**

   ➤ Review and discuss the two anxious experiences the child experienced (exposed himself to) during the week. Have him describe how he coped with the anxiety and how he rewarded himself. Reward the child's cooperation with points/stickers as appropriate. If the STIC was not completed, practice the anxious experiences planned for the STIC during today's session if possible.

   ➤ Ask the child to share his picture or cartoon (sci-fi) character drawing who can help him cope with his anxiety.

   ➤ Reward the child's cooperation with points/stickers as appropriate. If any part of the STIC was not completed, do it with the child at the start of the session or practice the anxious experience planned for the STIC during today's session if possible.

2. **Practice using exposure in high anxiety-provoking situations**

   For each exposure task practiced:

   ➤ Preparation FLEX

   In preparation for the exposure task, the therapist and child develop a FEAR plan for coping with the upcoming anxious situation (the plan can be entered on p. 36 in the workbook), thinking through what might and might not happen and preparing for the several more likely aspects of the event. The therapist and child negotiate a reward to be given if the child completes the exposure.

   FLEX

   ➤ Practice

   The therapist and child leave the office and go to a location in which the child can practice, in real life, the situation of moderate anxiety he has just role played/imagined. For example, gathering information (a survey) that requires talking to new people, purchasing something from a local store and being short a few cents, etc. Transportation, if necessary, is arranged prior to the session.

To present a coping model, the therapist remarks on aspects of the situation that might be generating anxiety. Covering each point in the FEAR plan, the therapist describes her thoughts and leaves open the opportunity for the child to comment or provide suggestions to help the therapist cope better. Importantly, in this out-of-the-office exposure task, the child collaborates with and helps the therapist use the steps of the FEAR plan.

The child is asked to describe his own feelings, somatic reactions, and anxious self-talk, as well as how to be adaptive. The therapist and child discuss appropriate coping strategies and reserve several minutes to do a relaxation exercise before and/or in the actual situation. Be sure to help the child develop actual strategies for coping within the situation and "think through" how to carry them out. If more than one aspect of the situation is troubling to the child, the therapist may want to address the different aspects separately.

Throughout the exposure task, the child provides a SUDS rating before and after the exposure as well as every minute along the way. The therapist records the child's SUDS rating and also rates how anxious she feels the child is, using the same scale at pre-, during (every minute), and post-exposure.

Following the exposure task, the child is rewarded for effort/completing the exposure task. The therapist and child process and discuss what the child found easiest and most difficult and develop ideas for further improvement. Emphasis is placed on what the child learned during the experience.

3.   **Plan exposure task(s) for Session 7**
   ➤ Using the situation cards/fear ladder in the *Brief Coping Cat Workbook* (pp. 53-54), the therapist and child decide on the situation that the child will

practice in Session 7. The situation that is selected is associated with high levels of anxiety.

4. **<u>Assign STIC task</u>**

    ➤ Ask the child to practice using the FEAR steps in three anxious situations that provoke moderate levels of anxiety and to record in his workbook what happened for discussion during the next session. When choosing practice exposure tasks, it is recommended to choose no more than one task that is expected to be time consuming for the child to do or for the parents to help arrange. Collaborate on a reward for the STIC tasks.

    ➤ Using the coping character the child cut out or created as part of the STIC for Session 5, the child is asked to make up a story about how that character could help other children cope in a situation like one that might make him feel anxious.

    ➤ Remind the child that there are only two more sessions!

Practicing in High Anxiety-Provoking Situations (Exposure Tasks)
Session 7

Purpose

Practice applying the skills for coping with anxiety in real (*in-vivo*) situations that produce high levels of anxiety in the child.

Goals

1. Review STIC task from Session 6
2. Practice using *in-vivo* exposure in high anxiety-provoking situations
3. Plan exposure task(s) for Session 8
4. Prepare for termination
5. Assign STIC task

Tasks

1.   **Review STIC task from Session 6**

➤ Discuss the two anxious experiences the child faced during the week. Have him describe how he coped with the anxiety, even if it went only partially well, and how he rewarded himself.

➤ Ask the child to share the story about his cartoon character who found himself in a scary situation. Discuss how successfully the character coped with his fears and worries. Reward the child's cooperation with points or stickers as appropriate. If part of the STIC was not completed, complete the story and/or practice the anxious experiences planned for the STIC during today's session if possible.

2.   **Practice using *in-vivo* exposure in high anxiety-provoking situations**

For each *in-vivo* exposure task practiced:

➤ Preparation FLEX

Discuss the anxious situation that was selected in Session 6 to practice in today's session. To prepare, the therapist and child develop a FEAR plan for coping with the upcoming anxious situation (the plan can be entered on p. 42 in the workbook), Think it though, processing with the child the experience that they are about to enter. Negotiate a reward to be given to the child for effort/completion of the task.

FLEX

➤ Practice

The therapist and child leave the office and go to a location in which the child can practice using the FEAR steps, in real life, in the situation of moderate anxiety he has just discussed with the therapist. Transportation, if necessary, is arranged prior to the session.

To present a coping model, the therapist remarks on aspects of the situation that might be generating anxiety and covers each point in the FEAR plan.

The child is asked to describe his own feelings, somatic reactions, and anxious self-talk, as well as how to better manage anxious arousal. The therapist and child discuss appropriate coping strategies and reserve a few minutes to do a relaxation exercise before and/or in the actual situation. Be sure to help the child develop actual strategies for coping within the situation and think through how to carry them out. Again, if more than one aspect of the situation is troubling to the child, the therapist addresses the different aspects separately.

As done in previous exposure tasks, the child provides a SUDS rating before and after the exposure as well as every minute during the exposure. The therapist records the child's SUDS rating and also provides a rating.

Following the exposure task the therapist guides an evaluation of the child's performance, discussing what the child found easiest and most difficult and what was learned. Help the child note even partial success on any or all parts of the FEAR plan. Ideas are developed for further improvement and the child is rewarded for effort/completing the *in-vivo* exposure task.

3.   **Plan exposure task(s) for Session 8**

➢ Using the situations cards/fear ladder in the *Brief Coping Cat Workbook* (pp. 53-54), the therapist and child decide on the situation that the child will face in Session 8. The situation is associated with high levels of anxiety; however, the therapist should help the client choose a task that the therapist is confident that the child can be successful at since this will be the child's final exposure; the exposure task could be a repeat exposure, a new high level exposure, or a moderate exposure, depending on the child's needs. Keep in mind that "high" refers to the child's level of anxiety in the exposure task, not the overall difficulty of the exposure task. Mention to the child that next week he will be using his coping skills in a challenging situation—maintain and encourage a positive, adventurous outlook.

4. **Address the facts that (a) therapy will be ending and (b) the relationship with the therapist will no longer be on a regular schedule.**

> This transition can be difficult for some clients. Children may begin to talk about increased anxiety and physical symptoms during the final weeks , almost suggesting a want for the session to continue. Informing the child at the end of each session (beginning at Session 6) how many sessions are left helps the child understand that his time with you is coming to an end. Encourage the child to talk about the end of therapy and help the child envision possible feelings that might occur during the last weeks or after the end of therapy. Applying the FEAR plan to this situation (e.g., worrying about how things will be without the therapist) is also suggested when the child shows signs of distress associated with terminating treatment.

> As the therapist, keep in mind that it is important to **provide ample support for the child in the belief that he is now ready to do well without the therapist.** Not perfect, but better. It is often a good idea to discuss possible upcoming difficult situations and how the child might handle these difficulties using the FEAR plan.

5. **Assign STIC task**

> Remind the child to practice using the FEAR steps in three anxious situations that provoke moderate levels of anxiety and to record in his workbook what happened for discussion during the next session. When choosing practice exposure tasks, it is recommended to choose no more than one task that is expected to be time consuming for the child to do or for the parents to help arrange. Arrange a reward for the STIC tasks.

> Remind the child that there is only one more session!

Practicing in High Anxiety Situations and Celebrating Success
Session 8

Purpose

Provide a final practice task applying the skills in an *in-vivo* exposure that produces high levels of anxiety in the child. Review and summarize the training program. Make plans with the parents to help the child maintain and generalize newly acquired skills. Bring closure to the therapeutic relationship.

Goals

1. Review STIC task from Session 7
2. Conduct a final exposure task in a challenging anxiety-provoking situation
3. Review and summarize the treatment program and bring closure to the therapeutic relationship

Tasks

1. **Review STIC task from Session 7**

   ➢ Review the anxious experiences the child was exposed to during the week, focusing on his autonomous efforts, his progress to date, and any special ways he has been able to become less anxious. As he describes how he coped with the anxiety and how he rewarded himself it can be helpful to applaud the improvements and share pride in the effort. At this juncture, the child is likely doing things that he could not do at the start of treatment. Reward the child appropriately. If the STIC was not completed during the past week, practice the anxious experiences planned for the STIC during today's session if possible.

2. **Conduct a final exposure task in a challenging anxiety-provoking situation**

   For each *in-vivo* exposure task practiced:

   ➢ Preparation FLEX

   Discuss the anxious situation selected in Session 7 to practice in today's session. Create a FEAR plan for coping with the anxious situation and enter it on p. 48 of the workbook. Keep in mind that we want this to be a successful experience for the child.

   FLEX

   ➢ Practice

   The therapist and child leave the office and go to a location in which the child can practice the situation just discussed using the FEAR plan, in real life. Transportation, if necessary, is arranged prior to the session. Because this is the final session, the exposure task is conducted at a nearby location so as to reserve time for review, a discussion of treatment termination, and some fun.

   As in past exposure tasks, the therapist can remark on aspects of the situation that might be generating anxiety in the child. However, it is good to have the child do this for himself. The child can describe his own feelings, somatic reactions, and anxious self-talk, as well as how to make it more adaptive. If the child wants to just "do it" and is moving forward (approaching) into the situation without distress, this can be supported. Importantly, the child is transitioned to take more of the lead in the use of the steps of the FEAR plan.

As in the past exposure tasks, gather SUDS ratings.

Following the final exposure task, think through and talk about the child's performance—note the progress since the start of treatment. Help the child note success on any or all parts of the FEAR plan. Discuss what the child has learned from engaging in this and previous exposure tasks.

4. **<u>Summarize the treatment program and bring closure to the relationship</u>**

➤ Recap with the parents and child what has been learned over the course of treatment. Review with the parents the "FEAR" acronym. Note that there have been gains but that there are areas still in need of improvement—this is always the case. During this review the therapist can help the child devise a couple advance "FEAR" plans for upcoming events.

➤ Encourage the parents to share their feedback about their child's progress and ask any questions or share any concerns that they may have about concluding treatment.

➤ Discuss relapse prevention with the parents and child. Describe for the parents (as was done with the child) that there may be times that are difficult in terms of coping with anxiety--this is normal. But, with continued practice there comes continued improvement. Given the expertise of the therapist, share any specific recommendations. These may include new ways for the parents to behave around their child (granting the child more autonomy) or situations in need of continued practice. The therapist discusses under what circumstance the family should consider additional treatment. If necessary, offer referrals for additional services (e.g., an obese child may want to try to lose weight). If fears remain, plan exposures for the child to practice in the coming month and discuss the importance of continued practice at home. The parents and child are given the therapist's card and are invited to call if they have questions/concerns, but they are also told to call to inform the therapist as to how the child is progressing. In short, the therapist invites further contact around future successes.

> The parents and child are given the therapist's card and are invited to call if they have any further questions/concerns, but they are also told to call to inform the therapist as to how the child is progressing. In short, the therapist invites further contact around future successes.

> Inform the parents that you will call to "check-in" and see how the child is doing. If appropriate, schedule a meeting for a posttreatment assessment and ask the parents to bring their current contact information for follow-up.

FLEX

> When the parents seem comfortable and satisfied with the discussion, ask them to leave for a few minutes so that you can share a "good-bye" with the child. When the parents have left the office, express your satisfaction with and encouragement for the child's efforts and present the child with a certificate (last page of the *Brief Coping Cat Workbook*) to commemorate completion of the treatment program. Have the certificate cosigned by an official (give the certificate added meaning, and provide an opportunity for another person to congratulate the child). During these moments, share some of the highlights of the therapy experience and ask the child to do the same. Begin to create the "history" of the treatment by talking about what has transpired. Encourage the child to continue to use what has worked for him and convey confidence in his ability to do so successfully. At the same time, point out that it is reasonable for there to be new situations and future times that may seem challenging. Remind the child that you will call in four weeks to talk about how he's doing.

Tips from the Trenches

Session 8

> During the last session, **provide the child with a final reward for participation** in the program. It is suggested that the reward be a social reward, such as playing a favorite game with the therapist, having a pizza "party" with the parents and therapist, going out for ice cream, or sharing some other activity. The time is set aside for having fun and the focus is kept on present and future accomplishments. The session may run longer than usual.

> An **end of treatment "commercial"** may be used to help the child summarize and demonstrate the knowledge that they learned during treatment. The therapist and child may work together to develop a song, picture, or demonstration of their accomplishments and knowledge attained during therapy. This "commercial" may be recorded. Parents may be invited to view the recording; sometimes, parents are included in making the "commercial." The content and quality of the video are less important than the celebratory context of the event: the child has come a long way and there is a recognition and reward for this progress. Parents may need to be guided to see the advances and not to harp on imperfections. Make a copy of the recording so that both the child and the therapist have one.

> The **therapist discusses with the child's parents how to support what has been learned** and to encourage use of the FEAR steps and willingness to try new tasks.

It is difficult to imagine any child whose problems are so circumscribed that they fit only the basic DSM or ICD criteria for a diagnosis of a specific anxiety disorder. Rather, many children who meet one set of diagnostic criteria often present with a variety of other symptoms as well (e.g., depression/dysthymia, hyperactivity, obsessions/compulsions, panic attacks).

In addition to problems of comorbidity, children may experience other complicating factors (e.g., realistic fears, family difficulties) and/or show behavior more directly connected to their primary anxiety disorder that could potentially interfere with treatment (e.g., hypercriticism, denial of anxiety, over-compliance and noncompliance, and school refusal). These instances require special attention.

Considered in this section are the special needs linked with various types of comorbidity and other complicating factors that may potentially impact treatment.

Comorbidity

> ### Depression/Dysthymia

The overlap between anxiety and depression is recognized (Brady & Kendall, 1992; Kendall, Brady, & Verduin, 2001; Kendall & Watson, 1989). Anxiety and depression share a number of symptoms, including irritability, agitation/restlessness, concentration difficulties, insomnia, and fatigue. Given this overlap, it is not surprising that a number of studies have revealed a high correlation between self-report measures of anxiety and depression (see Gotlib & Cane, 1989; Brady & Kendall, 1992). However, whereas there is a strong indication for the comorbidity of depression and anxiety in both children and adults (Angold, Costello, & Erkanli, 1999) , the degree to which they overlap remains in dispute.

One might expect that a number of children seeking treatment for anxiety problems may also be experiencing some depressive symptoms or a comorbid depressive disorder. It is the recognition of this possibility that prompts us to use a measure of depressive symptoms in our assessment: to be alert to depressive symptoms from the start of treatment. Research suggests that anxious youth with comorbid depression or co-occurring depressive symptoms may experience less favorable treatment outcomes than anxious youth without depression (Berman, Weems, Silverman, & Kurtines, 2000; Crawley, Beidas, Benjamin, Martin, & Kendall, 2008; O'Neil & Kendall, 2010). Thus, treatment modifications may be warranted to address the needs of anxious youth with comorbid depression or co-occuring depressive symptoms. In the course of considering the ways this treatment program can be modified to address depression, it is worthwhile to consider some of the similarities and differences, particularly at the emotional and cognitive level, which have been posited between depression and anxiety (see Kendall, Kortlander, Chansky & Brady, 1992).

Regarding differences at the emotional level, fear has been posited as a central component of anxiety whereas sadness has been considered central to depression (Izard, 1971). In addition, anxiety and depression have been differentiated along dimensions of the global constructs, negative and positive affect (Watson & Clark, 1984). Anxiety has been characterized as a state of negative affect (e.g., not excited, enthusiastic, or joyful; see Kendall & Watson, 1989). These findings suggest that while an anxious (but not depressed) child may experience a number of negative emotions, he/she may still have a relatively strong capacity for joy. On the other hand, a child who is both anxious and depressed may carry the double burden of experiencing a number of negative emotions with less hope of any relief offered by intermittent enjoyment.

The presence of depression has implications for the treatment of anxiety. First, because a cognitive-behavioral program involves a number of assignments that are done outside of the session, therapists may face a situation in which the dysphoric child's low motivation interferes with finishing these tasks. If the child is feeling hopeless, he may not see the value of completing the STIC assignments. The therapist moves the client along, offers the hope that she believes the child will feel less sad, and that completing the assigned task is one important step for feeling better. To sustain an atmosphere of hopefulness, the therapist is particularly encouraging about any attempts that are made to complete the tasks. Parents are an important resource (not interfering with the child and potentially encouraging the child throughout the week to complete the assignments). It is important that parents not be overbearing and inadvertently critical of their children's work. It is the case that some parents of children with anxiety problems have been overtly critical and judgmental, and this is also the case for dysphoric and depressed children. Helping parents to become supportive and encouraging, without "hovering," facilitates treatment progress.

Within each session, the therapist will want to emphasize "fun" activities; anxious children who are also dysthymic may have developed the habit of assuming they aren't going to have fun, so why try. For example, by engaging in various games (e.g., computer games or traditional board games) the child may be surprised that he is capable of engaging in a pleasurable activity. If deemed reasonable, the therapist may encourage parents to provide opportunities for fun at home.

Recognizing that he is capable of enjoying activities is tied to the child's implementing the fourth and final step in our "FEAR" acronym—Reward. With an increasing capacity for pleasure, the child will become more ready to think of ways of rewarding himself. Helping the dysphoric child discover means of self-reward is an important intervention in and of itself. Parents can be involved by pointing out times at home when the child can reward him/herself, as depressed and anxious children tend to focus on their mistakes and faults rather than accomplishments.

Working with an anxious child who is also somewhat depressed may entail addressing certain ongoing cognitive activities that are less likely to be found in a purely anxious child. Anxious children who are also depressed have cognition

70

associated with anxiety as well as typically depressogenic cognition: the more depressed cognition includes a greater emphasis on personal degradation and a greater preoccupation with the past. Because depressogenic attributions often involve focusing on past behavior as well as self-degradation for performance in past situations, depressive cognition can be addressed at the "E" (expectations), "A" (actions and attitudes), or "R" (results and rewards) step of the FEAR plan. In evaluating their performance in anxious situations, depressed children would be expected to make more internal attributions about negative outcomes than anxious children who are not depressed (see Kendall, Stark & Adam, 1990). By exploring these expectations and attributions for performance, therapists can help children become more aware and start to modify their dysfunctional thinking. Again, the therapist can involve the parents in addressing the child's depression. The therapist helps the parent to point out that feelings of depression are not permanent.

Conducting personal experiments, as used in treating depressed youth (see Lewinsohn & Clarke, 1999; Stark et al., 2006), resembles the collaborative empiricism of Beck's cognitive-behavioral therapy for depression (Beck, Rush, Shaw, & Emery, 1979; Hollon & Beck, 1979). In these "tests", clients are asked to describe situations and report their attributional conclusions. A shared experience with the therapist allows both the child and therapist to have some reasons for certain attributions, and the therapist can help the child think of ways to test such notions. For example, if the child and therapist have a shared interaction with another youth and the client thinks that the other child did not like him, the therapist would be able to ask "What made you think that?" and, possibly, "Is there any other way to explain it?" After related discussions and perhaps even further testing of such notions in which the child asks the other person if he liked or disliked him, the therapist and child work together to develop attributional patterns that are more consistent with the data and less biased by the depressed client's views about himself. To facilitate lasting cognitive change in the anxious and dysphoric child, the therapist can reward the child and tie the new causal attributions that have been generated into the "R" step of the FEAR program. The interested reader is referred to *Treating depressed children: Therapist manual for ACTION* (Stark, Schnoebelen, Simpson, Hargrave, Molnar, & Glenn, 2007).

➤ Hyperactivity

Although anxious children may exhibit signs of motor agitation (e.g., hair twisting, stuttering, wanting to leave an anxious situation; Barrios & Hartmann, 1997), hyperactive children are characterized by more impulsiveness (acting without thinking) in situations that require careful thinking (Kendall & Braswell, 1993). Given the high rates of comorbidity found between anxiety disorders and attention-deficit/hyperactivity disorder (ADHD; Costello, Mustillo, Erkanli, Keeler, & Angold, 2003), it is likely that clinicians will come in contact with children who exhibit both anxiety and hyperactivity. Fortunately, research suggests that anxious children with comorbid ADHD benefit from the *Coping Cat Program* at similar rates as anxious children without comorbid ADHD (Edmunds & Kendall, 2010; Flannery-Schroeder, Suveg, Safford, Kendall, & Webb, 2004; Hughes, Brown, & Kendall, 2010). These findings are likely dependent on the flexible adaptation of the *Coping Cat Program* for youth with ADHD. It is also the case that children receiving this program for anxiety may concurrently be receiving medications or other services for ADHD (e.g., Hinshaw, 2006).

In treating an anxious child who may also exhibit some signs of overactivity, the therapist can adjust both cognitive and behavioral parts of the current treatment program. At the behavioral level, the therapist may want to create a more structured approach to teaching the skills that are introduced during the first half of the program. Children with difficulties staying focused on task benefit from structured environments. In addition to discussing the agenda at the start of each session, it may be helpful for the clinician to write out the session agenda on a white board. This will orient the child to the task at hand and encourage on-task behavior. The child can then cross off each agenda item as it is accomplished. For children who have great difficulty staying on-task, the clinician may consider incorporating a token reinforcement system into the session structure such that the child earns points toward an end-of-session game for engaging in on-task behavior during each agenda item.

Anxious-overactive children may find it difficult to learn to relax. Because it may be anxiety provoking for these children to do muscle relaxation (see Heide & Borkovec, 1983; 1984 for a discussion of relaxation-induced anxiety), the skills might be introduced more gradually, with structure, and in terms of a game in which the child is told that he is learning to be a ragdoll. Specifically, the therapist can move around the room with the child telling him when to make various parts of his body like a ragdoll (i.e., relaxed) and when to make them like a robot (i.e., tensed). In this manner the therapist can participate as a coping model who shows that it is safe to become relaxed. Family members can serve as coping models as well. Rather than engaging in exercises for long intervals of time, the clinician can introduce and practice a variety of relaxation exercises for briefer periods of time.

It may also be helpful to oversee some of the STIC tasks—have the child draw pictures of anxiety-provoking situations in sessions or right after the sessions before he/she goes home, thus modeling and providing structure. This effort would be intended to prepare the child for the more concentration-demanding task of writing about anxiety producing situations in his *Brief Coping Cat Workbook*. With a hyperactive child, parents may need to be more involved in overseeing STIC tasks at home, by imposing structure or simply reminding the child.

Other aspects of the current treatment program lend themselves to working with children whose anxiety problems include some hyperactive patterns. A portion of this program involves the therapist's planning and modeling coping procedures. Repeated exposure to anxiety-related situations and "stopping to think" about how to cope with them may help the child reduce impulsivity and cope with anxiety. Overactive children have low levels of frustration tolerance and benefit from learning how to deal with failure without becoming excessively frustrated. We have often found it useful to model coping with making mistakes when working with anxious children who tend to see any error as indicative of personal failure. For instance, the therapist may intentionally fumble with audio equipment (when taping a session) and model a coping style of self-talk, in addition to modeling how to cope with the frustration of making a mistake. Again, parents and older siblings can also be coping models, disclosing mistakes or failure experiences and how they coped. This additional element of potential frustration in the face of making a mistake is added at the "E" of the FEAR steps as one of several cognitive facets in the situation that may be anxiety or frustration producing.

➤ Obsessive-Compulsive Patterns

Obsessional ruminations and compulsive ritualistic behavior has been seen as reflecting distressing levels of anxiety. There are children whose anxiety includes certain obsessive features (Henin & Kendall, 1997) and children who actually receive a diagnosis of obsessive compulsive disorder (Rapoport, 1986).

Because it is often thought that obsession and/or compulsions are anxiety-reducing for the sufferer, the child with such patterns may be highly resistant to changing them. The child may be quite rigid, hypervigilant, and even hostile about protecting this anxiety-reducing behavior because of a vague overwhelming fear of some disaster or harm befalling him. Individuals with obsessive compulsive disorder may not trust their feelings and perceptions about situations, and there is a strong tendency to avoid experiencing emotions if they are going to feel bad or out of control. The preferred way of treating obsessive compulsive disorder emphasizes exposing the individual to the anxiety-provoking situation without allowing the obsessive compulsive pattern to take place (response prevention). The individual is exposed to his/her anxiety at high levels. The FEAR plan can be applied to anxious situations that entail the obsessive compulsive behavior by creating exposure experiences (with response prevention) to address the obsessive compulsive difficulties. The therapist directs the parents in implementing response prevention strategies at home.

The severity of obsessive compulsive patterns varies greatly among the children. One distinction to keep in mind when deciding how to address such patterns is whether or not the pattern seems to represent a budding obsessive compulsive disorder or is rather a less severe byproduct of the perfectionism characteristic of perhaps an associated anxiety disorder (see Comer, Kendall, Franklin, Hudson, & Pimentel, 2004 for a discussion of the overlapping characteristics of obsessive compulsive patterns and generalized anxiety in children). To illustrate these possibilities, consider two examples of anxiety disordered children who have been treated in our clinic. In the case of a girl we'll call Maggie the therapist noticed that she was extremely perfectionistic. Overly concerned with making any type of error, she had difficulty completing the self-report forms in a timely fashion because she needed to check each page several times to make sure she had answered every question and queried any item for which she was not absolutely sure that the answer she gave was precise. In the second case, a client, we will call Sara, demonstrated a more extreme obsessive compulsive behavior pattern that interfered with her life. She was preoccupied with not being interrupted and, therefore, spoke very rapidly fearing that any break in her speech would result in an interruption.

Because Maggie's behavior appeared to be directly related to her overall perfectionism, rather than being a compulsion to check her answers, the problem was addressed within the framework of our program for youth with generalized anxiety. The therapist chose to set up an exposure task requiring the child to complete a

73

detailed task within certain time limits that would preclude excessive checking. In presenting the task, the therapist helped the child work through the FEAR steps so that she could cope with the anxiety that would arise in the face of possibly making an error that she did not have time to correct. Such experience, especially when repeated in various forms, helped the child to learn to be less perfectionistic, a common problem in generalized anxiety disorder.

For Sara, a more behavioral intervention, with somewhat less concern about use of the FEAR steps, seemed appropriate. Thus, the therapist asked Sara to engage in a conversation with someone who was instructed to interrupt her. It was anticipated that initially the child's anxiety would mount, but repeated experience with the situation would lead to extinction of the anxiety, and a concurrent reduction in the compulsion to speak very rapidly. Although our efforts did produce modest improvements, Sara did not complete the treatment program.

Because children with obsessive patterns are already extremely caught up in their own cognitive activity, attempts at cognitive exploration of the problem may backfire—leading to an escalation of their tendency to do too much thinking. A child whose overriding problem is obsessional thinking requires caution before undertaking a "heady" program. However, for a child whose primary problem is generalized anxiety with mild obsessive and/or compulsive features, the goal would be to reduce obsessive and/or compulsive patterns so that the anxiety that is related to the generalized anxiety can be fully addressed. When OCD is the primary problem, other systematic approaches should be considered (see Piacentini, March & Franklin, 2006).

➢ Panic Attacks

The child who experiences panic-like symptoms shows extreme concern for physiological responses associated with anxiety. There are a few children with a primary diagnosis of an anxiety disorder who also report panic-like symptoms such as a racing heart, shaking, chattering teeth, and dizziness. Additionally, ill-defined feelings of being overwhelmed have also been reported. Nelles and Barlow (1988) suggested that although children may manifest the physiological signs of panic, it is debatable whether prior to adolescence children are cognitively capable of making the internal attributions for their symptoms that are necessary for the cognitive component of panic attacks (e.g. "I'm going to die" [pg. 369]). Nelles and Barlow note that the incidence of diagnosed panic disorder in children is extremely low.

Despite the low incidence of childhood panic attacks, it is worthwhile to consider how the *Brief Coping Cat* program might be used to address these associated symptoms, even if they do not constitute a full panic attack. Because the panic-like symptoms can themselves be anxiety-provoking, it is appropriate to address them within the FEAR plan so that the child can learn to cope with such distressing physiological arousal. Such an approach entails helping the child identify what the initial physiological cues are that may spark the fear of experiencing intense physiological arousal. Having learned what responses typically foreshadow this arousal, a child can proceed to cope via the first of the FEAR steps—Feeling

Frightened? For instance, a child reports that a suddenly-racing heartbeat is his typical response before the general escalation of other physiological responses, and he learns to use this response as a cue to ask himself if he is feeling frightened. However, in the case of panic-like symptoms, the question would be used to identify whether the child was feeling frightened about the heart beat because it signaled the possibility of panic-like symptoms, or because of fear of some external circumstance. The child would then use the recently-acquired skills to "calm down." While taking deep breaths often works to initially calm anxiety, they may in the case of nascent panicky symptoms exacerbate hyperventilation which has been associated with the onset of panic (Ley, 1987). Thus, the child might want to focus on relaxing tense muscles instead.

Should the child's level of cognitive development permit, he might be encouraged to use the next step—"Expecting bad things to happen?" The child would be encouraged to focus on panic-related cognition: Is he expecting to lose control or is he fearing that he might be overwhelmed by the physiological symptoms and actually die? The goal of the first steps would be to nip in the bud the mounting physiological symptoms and the distorted thinking about these symptoms before the full-blown panic-like experience ensues. Because the escalation of physiological symptoms may be extremely rapid and intense, making the child aware of distorted thinking may be especially difficult; the therapist will have to be prepared to be particularly persistent in probing about this information. In the "Actions and Attitudes" step of the FEAR plan, the child can be encouraged to think of various ways to cope other than merely escaping from the arousing situation (such action readily reinforces avoidance behavior). Coping may involve the use of relaxation not only to prevent the anxiety but also to lower anxiety if it has begun to escalate (see Barlow & Cerny, 1988, for a cognitive-behavioral treatment of panic in adults). Coping may also include coping self-talk: "I know how to breathe; my body knows what to do".

The therapist may want to assess the parents' responses to the child's panicky symptoms. Parents may exacerbate the situation by being overreactive to the child's distress and by not allowing the child to cope independently. The family could role play an enactment of what happens when the child has a panicky reaction so that the therapist can notice how family members respond. The therapist can offer suggestions to parents about how they can handle the situation and they can role play this new behavior. If a parent is overreactive, the parent is encouraged to employ strategies to contain his/her own distress so that he/she can better help the child. Parents are directed to help the child implement his own coping strategies from the FEAR steps.

Other Complicating Factors

➤ **Problems with Compliance**

Anxious children are often concerned about pleasing others, and, in some instances, become overcompliant. Indeed, one of the reasons that anxious children often go without treatment is, unlike children with more externalizing symptoms (e.g., conduct disorder), anxious children's symptoms often result in compliance with others. The signs of overcompliance may include completing all STIC assignments perfectly as well as dutifully just going through the motions, afraid to question any assignments or express when he or she does not understand. The child may become anxious if he believes he has not done something exactly as it was supposed to have been done. One way to address this is for the therapist to encourage an instance of "noncompliance." For example, an overly compliant child (in fact, many of the clients) can be told that he must choose not to complete one of the STIC tasks (homework assignments). This slight deviation from doing what is expected may be very anxiety provoking. Yet, such a situation provides an opportunity for helping the overly-compliant child learn how to cope with anxiety when he misconstrues that something was done "wrong."

Though anxious children are often eager to please, occasionally children are reluctant to comply with the various activities involved in cognitive-behavioral treatment. Noncompliance can range from an out-right failure to complete the STIC tasks to passivity within the sessions. In trying to handle noncompliance, the therapist may want to ask what the behavior represents—what is the catastrophe that the child has thought of? For instance, a child may report that he is bored in the sessions and simply does not believe that there is very much in need of attention. However, such behavior may reflect a real fear of discussing very upsetting thoughts and feelings. A very intelligent 13-year-old girl, for example, felt ashamed that she was terrified whenever one of her parents was 15 minutes late after work. She had great difficulty opening up and telling the therapist that she imagined her parent to be dead.

Great patience and a willingness to try different approaches are needed in dealing with the noncompliant anxious child. Acknowledging that the child doesn't seem interested in what is being discussed, and following with probes about the reasons for this disinterest can be helpful. Asking the child how things might be better for him in the sessions, or an open recognition of some of the child's nonanxious emotions, such as anger or depression, are other possibilities. Extra efforts at rapport building may be required, such as finding a favorite activity (e.g., computer games) and using it during the session while at the same time accomplishing the session tasks. The goal is to strike a balance between making the noncompliant child aware that you empathize with the difficulty of discussing problems (and even their feelings that nothing is going to help), while at the same time projecting confidence that if they are willing to participate more thoroughly they really will be able to help themselves in difficult and painful situations.

➢ Hypercriticism

When working with an anxious child who is hypercritical the therapist can encourage and reward less-than-perfect performance on many STIC as well as in-session tasks. For instance, highly perfectionistic children fear doing anything that appears "sloppy." One little girl became upset when she accidentally got a pencil mark on a piece of paper on which she was about to draw. She immediately wanted to get a fresh sheet. The therapist asked her to use the original sheet and to use the FEAR steps to cope with appearing sloppy. The therapist explored the child's worries and fears—what might happen if she does something less than perfectly—particularly in reference to how they think others will perceive them. Hypercriticism can be addressed at the results and reward stage of the FEAR steps. These children find it very difficult to realistically assess their performance, seeing anything less than perfect as failure. One of the aims of the program is to help children realize that they do not have to perform perfectly in order to feel they have succeeded, and this point receives special emphasis when working with a hypercritical child.

Some parents of anxious children are hypercritical towards their own behavior or to that of the child. Thus, the parent's hypercriticism is a model for the child and reinforces the child's hypercriticism. The therapist can ask the parent to model recognition of their hypercritical behavior, and help them to more accurately assess their own performance. The parent can also model self-reward as it is not uncommon for the parent to have difficulty with this idea too. It is essential that the therapist help the parents to have realistic expectations of the child. The therapist can help the parents to modify the demands for perfect or overachieving behavior in their child.

➤ Denial of Anxiety

Anxious children may exhibit behavior that can interfere with treatment. This behavior is often related to their presenting problems. Among the most common is the initial denial of anxiety. For instance, consider the following: One of the instruments used to assess anxiety in children is a self-report questionnaire that asks the client how frequently he has difficulty making up his mind. The child is seated at a table and is reading and rereading the item. The alternatives are read and reread, and the therapist is approached with a question about the item. Even after the therapist has provided clarification, the child continues to labor over the item and "shows" genuine difficulty making up his mind. Eventually, after much consternation, the child reports that he does not have difficulty making up his mind. Thus, the questionnaire data (self-report) seems in contradiction to the observed actions. While it is only speculation, it seems that the child wants to present in a favorable manner (fake good) and has misinterpreted his own difficulties in making decisions to avoid reporting anxiety (see Kendall & Chansky, 1991).

More generally, it is not unusual for a child to be somewhat willing to report some anxious feelings during a diagnostic intake interview, only to report during an initial therapy session that he has no real problems with anxiety. More than likely, such denial represents the child's attempt to appear competent in the eyes of the therapist. It can be very helpful at such times for the therapist to disclose her own feelings of anxiety in certain situations. In addition, having family members disclose anxiety may also encourage the child to be more open. Such an approach normalizes the experience and can relieve the anxious child of the need to try to appear perfect and competent.

Sometimes, children actually exhibit several signs of anxiety (e.g., extreme hair twisting, nervous giggling, nervous motor activity) and yet when questioned whether they are feeling anxious, report no anxious feelings. This situation can be dealt with in several ways. The therapist may draw attention to the behavior and question; "I notice you're twisting your hair, I twist my hair when I'm nervous, do you?" It may be helpful again for the therapist to self-disclose as a coping model—showing how it can be easy to say you aren't anxious when you really are. This modeling can include statements about how it is difficult to get help coping with anxious feelings if people don't let anybody know how they are feeling. Another strategy is to have each family member report about a situation that makes another family member anxious. This exercise may help to normalize anxiety as each family member is described in an anxious situation. Having someone else report about a time the child was anxious may in this context allow the child to acknowledge at least some anxiety.

➢ School Refusal

Given the nature of school refusal, often families and/or schools are very desperate for solutions to the disruptions associated with the avoidance of school. The timing of the interventions, based on when the child's skills are in place and when the involved parties are ready to cooperate, is an important decision for the therapist. Attempting an intervention too soon can be detrimental (e.g., having the child attend school after an extended absence without first consulting the school staff). Similarly, a failure situation may be used by parents as evidence that the situation is unalterable and that other measures are needed (e.g., making the child switch to another school).

Specificity is often the key to success, thus the following guidelines are in the service of identifying the specific instances (contingencies) where school attendance difficulties arise, how they are currently being handled, and what strategies have been attempted unsuccessfully in the past.

Working with children who refuse school

First, it is necessary to identify why the child is refusing school, given that there school refusal is a heterogeneous pattern of behavior that overlaps with externalizing disorders such as oppositional defiant disorder (ODD) and attention deficit hyperactivity disorder (ADHD), as well as internalizing disorders such as anxiety and depression. Kearney and Albano (2000) described youth as those who refuse school to (a) avoid school-related objects or situations that cause distress or negative affect, (b) to escape aversive social and/or evaluative situations, (c) to receive attention from others outside of school, and/or (d) or to pursue reinforcement outside of school.

If a child is missing school due to anxious avoidance, then these recommendations apply (See Beidas, Crawley, Mychailyszyn, Comer, & Kendall, in press, for further recommendations). If the child is missing school due to other reasons (i.e., attention/reinforcement), then other interventions are necessary (e.g., behavior management/parent training; see Kearney & Albano, 2000).

We recommend implementation of a behavioral plan to keep the child in school from the beginning of treatment (i.e., from Session 1 or 2). Often separation anxiety and anxiety about particular situations at school co-occur, thus both problems need to be addressed in the treatment. This program is suited to address secondary school refusal in youth with primary anxiety disorders (Beidas et al., in press).

Children may be surprised, if not overwhelmed with all the attention the school avoidance has been receiving from angry teachers and parents alike. Therefore, while the therapist will be asking the child about school and other separation situations during Sessions 2-3 when discussing stressful situations, it is important that *other* low-stress situations be discussed as well. Conveying empathy for the child's situation is always important, but particularly when the child may be receiving negative, angry messages from adults in his life.

Early sessions involve learning about the types of school difficulties the child is having. Questions to consider include: Does the child have friends? Are there children teasing him? Is there a particular teacher of whom the child feels afraid? Does the child feel behind in any particular class due to absences? In general how is he feeling about his ability to keep up in school? How does the child cope with structured time (class time) versus unstructured time (recess, lunch, playing before school)?

Assessing strengths and resources is equally important. Is there a teacher or counselor at school with whom the child feels particularly safe? Are the child's friends in the same class? Are there some favorite activities which might be used as a reward for the child's courage and cooperation?

Importantly, once a plan has been established for the child to return to school, specific strategies need to be developed with the child. For example, if the child is feeling upset in the morning or on the walk to school or during class, what can he do? A child survival pack of stickers, helpful positive thoughts, or strategies (e.g., making eye contact with a friend) can be brought to school as tangible reminders of the child's coping mechanisms. A reward such as making contact with a favorite teacher or counselor at the end of the day is arranged. Depending on the age of the child, the parents can be told of the child's own plan so that they may help the child to remember to use it. If the child cries, has outbursts, or in some way disrupts the classroom, an additional option may be to have a room or space away from the class where the child can sit quietly for a few minutes to collect himself. This "pause" can include contact with a teacher or counselor, but should be firmly time-limited and geared toward the next step of getting back to class (See teacher interventions below).

Working with parents of youth who refuse school

The first step when working with parents of school avoidant youth is to learn more about how the school avoidance has developed and exactly how it has been handled in the past. This will include exploration of any difficulties at home which may be of concern to the child (e.g., abuse, alcoholism). A non-threatening question can be asked to assess this: "Though we are a child-focused treatment, we need to be aware of any situations in the child's life which may be worrying him or interfering with his day-to-day activities—whether this be in the home (any illnesses or conflict) or in the neighborhood (crime)." After assessing any potential "parent" problems, the therapist discusses how these problems might interfere with the child's treatment, and discuss options (e.g., referring the parents for treatment) to address these problems. General information-gathering includes answers to such questions as "How long has this problem been going on?" "In what ways does it interfere in the child's life?" "When does the child first start to protest school (night before, morning of)?" "How does the child protest—crying, stomachaches, temper tantrums?" "Which parent typically responds and how?" "How does the parent get the child to school?" "When does the parent "concede" the fight, i.e., when do you let the child stay home?" "How do parents work together or against each other?" "How does each think the situation should be handled?" Answers to these questions help the therapist be proactive in developing a plan that will prevent possible failure. For example, a plan will be undermined if a parent is unable to bear hearing their child say "My stomach is coming apart and I'm gonna die," and knowing this allows the therapist to help the parent plan to cope with the distress. The therapist supports the parent in how difficult it can be is to hear their child upset, but offers direction—hug the child and say you are sorry the child is not feeling well but that it's time to go to school.

Discuss parents' fears. The therapist may need to discuss parent fears at length, until parents are clearly reassured that making their child go to school is both developmentally appropriate (they're not asking their child to do anything that other children their age could not do) and a positive parental responsibility. The parents are advised that the transition may be difficult for them, but that their child does want to grow up and go to school. Set the expectation that upset, crying, and hurt feelings may be part of the process and that they should not be afraid of the initial distress: reassure parents that their children will know that they still love them—and that the children need their help in solving this problem. The therapist conveys her belief that this problem is manageable and that success is imminent as long as everyone keeps to the plan.

Sometimes a written agreement is provided for parents. The written information describes how to get the child to school—verbal encouragements, supportive statements, and firm directions to get the child ready for school and for being dropped off at school (or at the bus). For example, if a child is yelling (or crying) at home in the morning, the parents have the written suggestions to acknowledge the distress, give verbal support, but continue to help the child get dressed or get breakfast, etc.

Shaping can be used. It may be worthwhile during the first few days of the plan to drop the child off immediately prior to the start of class rather than 15 minutes prior to school. The unstructured time before class begins may be too difficult for the child to manage. During the second or third week if the child is ready, earlier arrival can be incorporated.

The "R" of the FEAR plan (Results and rewards) is central to success. Explain the value of "reward" to the parents, how it helps increase desired behavior and makes the child feel proud. Rewarding can be fun—parent and child making a chart and choosing rewards. Each day the child earns credit (sticker, points) for going to school, with the expectation that the child will attend school each of the five days and get the preferred reward. With the help of the therapist, parents are encouraged to praise the child when school is attended and the points are awarded and, if the child does not go to school, to refrain from assigning points, but do not punish the child or draw attention to the situation. For example, parents are specifically told and given opportunity to practice not taunting the child: "See, you didn't get any stars today, you're not going to get your reward." If the child doesn't go to school, the parents do not assign the points, phone the therapist and discuss what went wrong, and make a plan for how to get back on track.

Arrangements for the reward are made in advance. Often parents are reluctant to reward their children for something that the parents think they should do for nothing. Parents may feel resentful, "I never got a reward for going to school." These concerns must be addressed, otherwise parents may undermine the reward and thus the overall plan. Have parents somewhat involved in the selection of the reward—in other words, within their price range or time constraints. Explain to parents that the return to school is challenging and scary for their child and although they will not be required forever, rewards will help solve the problem at this time. Also, assure them that once the child is back at school, the rewards will be faded out. It is worth noting that, often, separation anxious children are happy with non-monetary rewards such as spending special time with parents.

Working with the school personnel of youth who refuse school

Working with youth who refuse school benefits from coordinated efforts with teachers, counselors, and school principals. Begin with information gathering from key individuals (e.g., teacher or counselor) and find out what other school personnel may be involved in the school avoidance. This may include the school nurse, for example, who sends the child home from school when he complains of stomachaches. Maintain a stance that is cooperative and supportive. Find out how the avoidance has been problematic for the school and learn what resources the school has. For example, a teacher may know of a "buddy" to link the child up with to help the child feel comfortable in school, or may have access to rewards for the child.

Useful questions for the school personnel include: "What is the school's stance about the problem?" "How long has the problem been going on?" "Does the child have difficulty 1st thing in the morning?" "After certain classes?" "How has the school been handling the problem?" (find out the exact contingencies). "Is the child spending time in the nurse's office or the counselor's office?" "Is the child sent home often?" "What is a reasonable system for managing the child's distress?" "Is there a place where the child can go for 2-3 minutes to collect himself before returning to the classroom?"

➢ Realistic Fears

Therapists need to be sensitive to the reality basis of a child's distress. Children from low SES groups have been found to have more fears about specific events or things—perhaps resulting from the reality that their environments contain more threatening events. Such first hand experiences with very threatening situations, situations that children in other circumstances would simply never have to face, can result in detrimental anxiety. For example, one of our adolescent clients had a fear of being stabbed; as it turned out she had actually been stabbed and had seen others being stabbed during various street fights. Stressful and threatening environments contributing to the child's anxiety are not limited to children from low SES backgrounds. Children from various SES groups may live in chaotic homes where there is a relative lack of parental support because the parents themselves are under great stress (e.g., from work, marital problems, being a single parent, or illness).

At a pragmatic level, a disorganized home environment may create difficulties for treatment effectiveness in terms of lost relaxation tapes, notebooks, or other session related materials. Likewise the child may have trouble completing schoolwork, which in turn may contribute to his anxiety about school performance. On an emotional level, parents who are under stress may at times be somewhat unpredictable. Thus, for example, one 12-year-old boy suffered a great deal of anxiety about being hurt by bigger children. In somewhat ambiguous situations, such as being bumped in the hall at school during the crowded rush to classes, he would perceive the other children as trying to harm him. The origins of these fears became clearer when, during the parent session, the mother reported that the father, who was currently working two jobs, was presently very moody and unpredictable in his behavior toward the child, at times lashing out and hitting him for only minor transgressions. Similarly, if a parent is him/herself experiencing extreme anxiety and presenting the world as a threatening place to the child, the child's fear may be grounded in the fear-filled "reality" that is presented by the parent. The therapist needs to be sensitive to the parent's anxiety, but the focus of treatment is on helping the child learn to recognize realistic fears and stressful circumstances and to identify strategies to cope with them. An integral part of this involves helping the child learn to distinguish between what are reality-based fears and what fears and worries result from misinterpretation or over generalization of situations which are similar to fearful situations that the child actually faces (e.g., the threat of an unpredictable father versus being bumped in the school hall).

➢ Family Difficulties

The present program is geared toward helping the child to cope with his anxiety. The problems described so far have been problems that children might bring into treatment. Although we have mentioned ways parents might contribute to or maintain the child's difficulty and how they can be encouraged to help the child, parents and other family members also may create difficulties to the therapeutic process.

One of the goals of the program is to consider family factors that may be maintaining the child's difficulties. Common problems may include parents who are overly critical or overprotective, and inappropriate limit setting. These factors will be addressed as part of the therapy process. However, in some cases, children will be learning the FEAR steps, but the parents will not be receptive to the therapist's input regarding changes they need to make. To encourage receptiveness on the part of parents, therapists need to take care that parents do not feel unduly blamed or criticized. Their strengths as parents need to be emphasized as well as their potential weaknesses.

In some cases, parents may try to monopolize time to discuss their own problems that are not directly relevant to the child's anxiety. Though the therapist needs to be compassionate, the therapist also needs to keep the therapy on track and goal oriented and redirect the parents to the task at hand. For example, if a parent is overly identified with the child and constantly talks about his/her own anxiety, this information can be incorporated into the exposure sessions, the therapist would emphasize the distinction between the parent's feelings and the child's. In other cases, parents or siblings will bring up completely unrelated material such as work problems. If necessary, the therapist may spend a portion of separate time with the parents to address issues and consider making outside referrals for the parents.

Parental psychopathology, substance abuse, or marital problems all may negatively impact on the therapy process because the parents may be less motivated, or less able to change behavior that contributes to or maintains the child's difficulty. In any of these instances, the therapist tries to capitalize on strengths in the family or ways that one or more family members can compensate for problems.

If a parent is depressed, for example, the parent may have difficulty following through on out-of-session suggestions. A parent's depression may serve to reinforce a negative attributional style in the child through modeling, and may diminish positive reinforcement of the child by the parent. Depression may also contribute to marital difficulties, and marital conflict can have a negative effect on the child as well.

If there are marital problems, one parent may be less invested in helping the child overcome anxiety. It is not uncommon to find that when a separation anxious child sleeps in the parent's bed, marital problems help to maintain the behavior. The therapist has to encourage the parents to work together in helping the child. However, at times, if one parent has serious psychological problems which contribute to a difficult relationship with the child, encouraging the other parent to become more involved with the child may lessen the stress in the family as long as this involvement does not cause the child-parent alliance to be stronger than the marital alliance.

If a parent tends to lash out at the child when the parent is stressed, the therapist can help the family to identify the warning signs and have them use the FEAR plan to think of different ways of handling the situation. The child's role play may include a parent who acts out different ways on handling a stressful situation, with the therapist's help. The plan may simply involve recognition of the warning signals and the parent and child going to different parts of the house until the parent cools off. The parent may be able to use relaxation exercises to calm him/herself.

Substance abuse on the part of a parent can also create difficulties in treatment. In some cases, the family will keep the substance abuse hidden, and the therapist may sense that there is a secret. In such cases, it may be easier for the parents to reveal this problem in a separate meeting with the therapist.

Closing Comments

Although this manual allows for the flexibility needed to deal with children who have a variety of problems, the primary and principal focus is on helping children learn how to manage and cope with distressing anxiety. Thus, in assessing whether or not a child's problems are amenable to treatment within a cognitive-behavioral framework, one must consider how much the child's general functioning will be helped if he learns to cope more successfully with anxiety. In making such a decision, it may be helpful to conceptualize potential difficulties in treatment as lying along a continuum, ranging from symptoms of anxiety to the presence of other disorders. Some problems, such as hypercriticism or overcompliance, may be products of the child's fundamental anxiety. Other problems, such as comorbid depression, obsessive compulsive patterns, or hyperactivity, involve a more complex situation that may relate to functional difficulties outside the realm of anxiety. In general, the degree to which the program will likely be useful for children displaying symptoms of other disorders and for children in families with significant problems besides the child's anxiety will vary with the individual child and his family and the skill of the therapist. Our goal associated with the previous suggestions is to help determine how best to approach potential difficulties in treatment and help facilitate flexible applications of a structured intervention. Therapist supervision provides opportunities for discussing these and other potential difficulties. It is urged that therapists have access to supportive and encouraging supervision on a regular basis.

References

Angold, A., Costello, E. J., & Erkanli, A. (1999). Comorbidity. *Journal of Child Psychology and Psychiatry, 40,* 57-87.

Barlow, D., & Cerny, J. (1988). *Psychological treatment of panic.* New York: Guilford Press.

Barrett P., Dadds, M., & Rapee, R. (1996). Family treatment of childhood anxiety: A controlled trial. *Journal of Consulting and Clinical Psychology, 64,* 336-342.

Barrios, B., & Hartmann, D. (1997). Fears and anxieties. In E. Mash and L. Terdal (Eds.). *Assessment of childhood disorders* (3rd ed., pp. 196-264) New York: Guilford.

Beck, A. T., Rush, A., Shaw, B., & Emery, G. (1979). *Cognitive therapy of depression.* New York: Guilford Press.

Beidas, R.S., Benjamin, C.L., Puleo, C.M., Edmunds, J.M., & Kendall, P.C. (2010). Flexible applications of the Coping Cat program for anxious youth. *Cognitive and Behavioral Practice, 17,* 142-153.

Beidas, R.S., Crawley, S., Mmychailyszyn, M., Comer, J., & Kendall, P.C. (in press). Cognitive behavioral treatment of anxious youth with comorbid school refusal in a university based clinic: Clinical presentation and treatment response. *Psihologijske Teme (Psychological Topics).*

Beidas, R.S., Podell, J.L., and Kendall, P.C. (2008). Cognitive-behavioral treatment for child and adolescent anxiety: The Coping Cat Program. In C.L LeCroy (Ed.), Handbook of Evidence Based Treatment Manuals for Children and Adolescents (2nd ed.). New York: Oxford University Press.

Berman, S. L., Weems, C. F., Silverman, W. K., & Kurtines, W. M. (2000). Predictors of outcome in exposure-based cognitive and behavioral treatments for phobic and anxiety disorders in children. *Behavior Therapy, 31,* 713-731.

Brady, E., & Kendall, P. C. (1992). Comorbidity of anxiety and depression in children and adolescents. *Psychological Bulletin, 111,* 244-255.

Chambless, D., & Hollon, S. (1998). Defining empirically supported treatments. *Journal of Consulting and Clinical Psychology, 66,* 5-17.

Chansky, T. E., & Kendall, P. C. (1997). Social expectations and self-perceptions of children with anxiety disorders. *Journal of Anxiety Disorders, 11,* 347-365.

The Child Anxiety Network (2001). *I Can Relax! Relaxation CD for Children.* http://childanxiety.net/.

Chu, B.C. & Kendall, P.C. (2004). Positive association of child involvement and treatment outcome within a manual-based cognitive-behavioral treatment for anxious youth. *Journal of Consulting and Clinical Psychology, 72,* 821-829.

Comer, J., Kendall, P.C., Franklin, M., Hudson, J. & Pimentel, S. (2004). Obsessing/worrying about the overlap between obsessive-compulsive disorder and generalized anxiety disorder in youth. *Clinical Psychology Review, 24,* 663-683.

Costello, E. J., Mustillo, S., Erkanli, A., Keeler, G., & Angold, A. (2003). Prevalence and development of psychiatric disorders in childhood and adolescence. *Archives of General Psychiatry, 60,* 837-844.

Crawley, S., Beidas, R., Benjamin, C., Martin, E., & Kendall, P. C. (2008). Treating socially phobic youth with CBT: Differential outcomes and treatment considerations. *Behavioural and Cognitive Psychotherapy, 36,* 379-389.

Creed, T.A. & Kendall, P.C. (2005). Empirically supported therapist relationship-building behavior within a cognitive–behavioral treatment for anxiety in youth. *Journal of Consulting and Clinical Psychology.*

Edmunds, J. M., & Kendall, P. C. (2010). Externalizing comorbidity, in-session externalizing behavior, and outcome in youth treated for anxiety disorders. Manuscript in preparation.

Fauber, R., & Kendall, P. C. (1992). Children and families: Integrating the focus of interventions. *Journal of Psychotherapy Integration, 2,* 107-124.

Flannery-Schroeder, E., & Kendall, P. C. (1996). *Cognitive behavioral therapy for anxious children: Therapist manual for group treatment.* Ardmore, PA: Workbook Publishing.

Flannery-Schroeder, E., Suveg, C., Safford, S., Kendall, P. C., & Webb, A. (2004). Comorbid externalizing disorders and child anxiety treatment outcomes. *Behaviour Change, 21,* 14-25.

Gotlib, I., & Cane, D. (1989). Self-report assessment of depression and anxiety. In P. C. Kendall & D. Watson (Eds.), *Anxiety and depression: Distinctive and overlapping features* (pp. 131-169). New York: Academic Press.

Heide, F., & Borkovec, T. (1983). Relaxation-induced anxiety: Paradoxical anxiety enhancement due to relaxation training. *Journal of Consulting and Clinical Psychology, 51,* 171-182.

Heide, F., & Borkovec, T. (1984). Relaxation-induced anxiety: Mechanisms and theoretical implications. *Behavior Research and Therapy, 22,* 1-12.

Henin, A., & Kendall, P. C. (1997). Obsessive compulsive disorder in children and adolescents. In T. H. Ollendick & R. J. Prinz (Eds.) *Advances in clinical child psychopathology* (vol. 19, pp. 75-131). New York: Plenum Press.

Hinshaw, S. (2006). Attention-deficit/hyperactivity disorder. In P. C. Kendall (Ed.) (3rd edition), *Child and adolescent therapy: Cognitive-behavioral procedures.* New York: Guilford Press.

Hollon, S., & Beck, A. T. (1979). Cognitive therapy of depression. In P.C. Kendall & S. Hollon (Eds.), *Cognitive-behavioral interventions: Theory, research, and procedures* (pp. 153-203). New York: Academic Press.

Howard, B., Chu, B.C., Krain, A., Marrs-Garcia, A., & Kendall, P.C. (2000). *Cognitive-behavioral family therapy for anxious children: Therapist manual.* Ardmore, PA: Workbook Publishing.

Howard, B., & Kendall, P. C. (1996). Cognitive-behavioral family therapy for anxiety-disordered children: A multiple-baseline evaluation. *Cognitive Therapy and Research, 20,* 423-444.

Hudson, J., Krain, A., & Kendall, P. C. (2001). Expanding horizons: Adapting manual-based treatments for anxious children with comorbid diagnoses, *Cognitive and Behavioral Practice, 8,* 338-346.

Hughes, A. A., Brown, R. T., & Kendall, P. C. (2010). Treatment outcomes for children with anxiety disorders and comorbid attention-deficit hyperactivity disorder. Manuscript submitted for publication.

Izard, C. (1971). *The face of emotion.* New York: Appleton-Century-Crofts.

Kazdin, A. E., & Weisz, J. (1998). Identifying and developing empirically supported child and adolescent treatments. *Journal of Consulting and Clinical Psychology, 66,* 19-36.

Kearney, C.A., and Albano, A.M (2007). *When children refuse school: A cognitive-behavioral therapy approach (2nd edition).* New York, NY: Oxford University Press.

Kendall, P. C. (2006). Guiding theory. In P. C. Kendall (Ed.), *Child and adolescent therapy: Cognitive-behavioral procedures* (3rd ed.). New York: Guilford.

Kendall, P.C. (1992). *The Coping cat workbook.* Ardmore, PA: Workbook Publishing.

Kendall, P. C. (1993). Cognitive-behavioral therapies with youth: Guiding theory, current status, and emerging developments. *Journal of Consulting and Clinical Psychology, 61,* 235-247.

Kendall, P. C. (1994). Treating anxiety disorders in youth: Results of a randomized clinical trial. *Journal of Consulting and Clinical Psychology, 62,* 100-110.

Kendall, P. C., Brady, E. U., & Verduin, T. L. (2001). Comorbidity in childhood anxiety disorders and treatment outcome. *Journal of the American Academy of Child and Adolescent Psychiatry, 40,* 787-794.

Kendall, P. C., & Braswell, L. (1993). *Cognitive-behavioral therapy for impulsive children (2nd ed.).* New York: Guilford Press.

Kendall, P. C., & Chansky, T. E. (1991). Considering cognition in anxiety-disordered children. *Journal of Anxiety Disorders, 5,* 167-186.

Kendall, P.C., Choudhury, M.A., Hudson, J., & Webb, A. (2002). The C.A.T. Project Manual. Ardmore, PA: Workbook Publishing.

Kendall, P. C., & Chu, B. C. (2000). Retrospective self-reports of therapist flexibility in a manual-based treatment for youths with anxiety disorders. *Journal of Clinical Child Psychology, 29,* 209-220.

Kendall, P. C., Chu, B., Gifford, A., Hayes, C., & Nauta, M. (1999). Breathing life into a manual: flexibility and creativity with manual-based treatments. *Cognitive and Behavioral Practice, 5,* 177-198.

Kendall, P. C., Flannery-Schroeder, E., Panichelli-Mindel, S., Southam-Gerow, M., Henin, A., & Warman, M. (1997). Therapy for youths with anxiety disorders: A second randomized clinical trial. *Journal of Consulting and Clinical Psychology, 65,* 366-380.

Kendall, P.C., Podell, J., & Gosch, E. (2010). *The Coping cat: Parent companion.* Ardmore, PA: Workbook Publishing.

Kendall, P. C., Gosch, E., Furr, J. M., & Sood, E. (2008). Flexibility within fidelity. *Journal of the American Academy of Child and Adolescent Psychiatry, 47,* 987-993.

Kendall, P.C., & Hedtke, K.A. (2006). *Cognitive-behavioral therapy for anxious children: Therapist manual (3rd edition).* Ardmore, PA: Workbook Publishing.

Kendall, P.C., & Hedtke, K.A. (2006). *The Coping cat workbook (2nd edition).* Ardmore, PA: Workbook Publishing.

Kendall, P. C. & Holmbeck, G. (1991). Psychotherapeutic interventions for adolescents. In R. Lerner, A. Peterson, & J. Brooks-Gunn (Eds.), *The encyclopedia of adolescence* (pp. 866-874). New York: Garland Publishing.

Kendall, P.C., Hudson, J., Choudhury, M., Webb, A. & Pimentel, S. (2005b). Cognitive-behavioral treatment for childhood anxiety disorders. In E. D. Hibbs & P. S. Jensen (Eds.) *Psychosocial treatments for child and adolescent disorders:*

Empirically based strategies for private practice (pp. 47-74). Washington, DC: American Psychological Association.

Kendall, P. C., Hudson, J., Gosch, E., Flannery-Schroeder, E., & Suveg, C. (2008). Cognitive-behavioral therapy for anxiety disordered youth: A randomized clinical trial evaluating child and family modalities. *Journal of Consulting and Clinical Psychology, 76,* 282-297.

Kendall, P. C. & Khanna, M. (2008). *Camp Cope-A-Lot: The coping cat CD.* Ardmore, PA: Workbook Publishing.

Kendall, P.C., & Khanna, M. (2008). *CBT4CBT: Computer-based training to be a cognitive-behavioral therapist.* United States: Workbook Publishing.

Kendall, P. C., Kortlander, E., Chansky, T. E., & Brady, E. U. (1992). Comorbidity of anxiety and depression in youth: Treatment implications. *Journal of Consulting and Clinical Psychology, 60,* 869-880.

Kendall, P. C. & Macdonald, J. P. (1993). Cognition in the psychopathology of youth, and implications for treatment. In K. S. Dobson and P. C. Kendall (Eds.), *Psychopathology and cognition* (pp. 387-427). San Diego: Academic Press.

Kendall, P.C., Robin, J.A., Hedtke, K.A., Gosch, E., Flannery-Schroeder, E., & Suveg, C. (2005a). Conducting CBT with anxious youth? Think exposures. *Cognitive and Behavioral Practice, 12,* 136-148.

Kendall, P.C., Safford, S., Flannery-Schroeder, E., & Webb, A. (2004). Child anxiety treatment: Outcomes in adolescence and impact on substance use and depression at 7.4-year follow-up. *Journal of Consulting and Clinical Psychology, 72,* 276-287.

Kendall, P. C., & Southham-Gerow, M. A. (1995). Issues in the transportability of treatment: The case of anxiety disorders in youths. *Journal of Consulting and Clinical Psychology, 63,* 702-708.

Kendall, P. C., & Southam-Gerow, M. A. (1996). Long-term follow-up of a cognitive-behavioral therapy for anxiety-disordered youth. *Journal of Consulting and Clinical Psychology, 64,* 724-730.

Kendall, P. C., Stark, K. D., & Adam, T. (1990). Cognitive deficit or cognitive distortion in childhood depression. *Journal of Abnormal Child Psychology, 18,* 255-270.

Kendall, P. C., & Treadwell, K. R. H. (1996). Cognitive-behavioral treatment for childhood anxiety disorders. In P. S. Jensen & E. D. Hibbs (Eds.), *Psychosocial treatment research with children and adolescents* (pp. 23-42). Washington, DC: APA.

Kendall, P. C., & Warman, M. J. (1996). Anxiety disorders in youth: Diagnostic consistency across DSM-III-R and DSM-IV. *Journal of Anxiety Disorders, 10,* 453-463.

Kendall, P. C., & Watson, D. (Eds.). (1989). *Anxiety and depression: Distinctive and overlapping features.* NY: Academic.

Khanna, M. & Kendall, P. C. (2010). Computer-assisted cognitive-behavioral therapy for child anxiety: Results of a randomized clinical trial. *Journal of Consulting and Clinical Psychology*, in press.

Koeppen, A. S. (1974). Relaxation training for children. *Elementary School Guidance and Counseling, 9,* 14-21.

Kortlander, E., Kendall, P. C., & Panichelli-Mindel, S. (1997). Maternal expectations and attributions about coping in anxious children. *Journal of Anxiety Disorders, 11,* 297-315.

Krain, A., Hudson, J., Coles, M. & Kendall, P. C. (2002). The case of Molly L: Use of family cognitive-behavioral treatment for childhood anxiety. *Clinical Case Studies, 1,* 271-298.

Lewinsohn, P. M., & Clarke, G. (1999). Psychosocial treatments for adolescent depression. *Clinical Psychology Review, 19,* 329-342.

Ley, R. (1987). Panic disorder. In L. Michelson & M. Ascher (eds.) *Anxiety and stress disorders: Cognitive-behavioral assessment and treatment.* New York: Guilford Press.

Nelles, W., & Barlow, D. (1988). Do children panic? *Clinical Psychology Review, 8,* 359-372.

O'Neil, K. A., & Kendall, P. C. (2010). Role of comorbid depression and co-occurring depressive symptoms in outcomes for anxiety-disordered youth treated with cognitive-behavioral therapy. Manuscript submitted for publication.

Ollendick, T. H., & Cerny, J. A. (1981). *Clinical behavior therapy with children.* New York: Plenum Press.

Ollendick, T. H., & King, N. (1998). Empirically supported treatments for children with phobic and anxiety disorders. *Journal of Clinical Child Psychology, 27,* 156-167.

Ollendick, T. H., King, N., & Chorpita, B. (2006). Empirically-supported treatments for children. In P. C. Kendall (Ed.) (3rd edition), *Child and adolescent therapy: Cognitive-behavioral procedures.* New York: Guilford Press.

Piacentini, J., March, J., Franklin, M. (2006). Cognitive-behavioral therapy for youngsters with obsessive-compulsive disorder. In P. C. Kendall (Ed.) (3rd edition), *Child and adolescent therapy: Cognitive-behavioral procedures.* New York: Guilford Press.

Podell, J.L., Mychailszyn, M., Edmunds, J.M., Puleo, C.M., & Kendall, P.C. (2010). The Coping Cat program for anxious youth: The FEAR plan comes to life. *Cognitive and Behavioral Practice, 17,* 132-141.

Rapoport, J. (1986). Childhood obsessive compulsive disorder. *Journal of Child Psychology and Psychiatry, 27,* 289-295.

Ronan, K., Kendall, P. C., & Rowe, M. (1994). Negative affectivity in children: Development and validation of a self-statement questionnaire. *Cognitive Therapy and Research, 18,* 509-528.

Silverman, W. K., Pina, A. A., Viswesvaran, C. (2008). Evidence-based psychosocial treatments for phobic and anxiety disorders in children and adolescents. *Journal of Clinical Child and Adolescent Psychology, 37,* 105-130.

Southam-Gerow, M., & Kendall, P. C. (2000). A preliminary study of the emotion understanding in youth referred for treatment of anxiety disorders. *Journal of Clinical Child Psychology, 29,* 319-327.

Stark, K., Hargrave, J., Sander, J., Custer, G., Schnoebelen, S., Simpson, J., & Molnar, J. (2006). Treatment of childhood depression: The ACTION treatment program. In P. C. Kendall (Ed.) (3rd edition), *Child and adolescent therapy: Cognitive-behavioral procedures.* New York: Guilford Press.

Stark, K. D., Schnoebelen, S., Simpson, J., Hargrave, J., Molnar, J., & Glenn, R. (2007). *Treating depressed youth: Therapist manual for ACTION.* Ardmore, PA: Workbook Publishing.

Suveg, C., Comer, J., Furr, J., & Kendall, P. C. (2006). Adapting manualized CBT for a cognitively-delayed child with multiple anxiety disorders. *Clinical Case Studies.*

Treadwell, K. R. H., & Kendall, P. C. (1996). Self-talk in anxiety-disordered youth: States-of-mind, content specificity, and treatment outcome. *Journal of Consulting and Clinical Psychology, 64,* 941-950.

Treadwell, K. R. H., Flannery, E. C., & Kendall, P. C. (1995). Ethnicity and gender in relation to adaptive functioning, diagnostic status, and treatment outcome in children from an anxiety clinic. *Journal of Anxiety Disorders, 9,* 373-384.

Walkup, J., Albano, A. M., Piacentini, J., Birmaher, B., Compton, S., Sherrill, J., et al. (2008). Cognitive-behavioral therapy, sertraline and their combination for children and adolescents with anxiety disorders: Acute phase efficacy and safety: The Child/Adolescent Anxiety Multimodal Study (CAMS). *New England Journal of Medicine, 359,* 2753-2766.

Watson, D., & Clark, L. (1984). Negative affectivity: The disposition to experience negative emotional states. *Psychological Bulletin, 96,* 465-490.

ISBN: 978-1-888805-49-9